Lake Superior Journal
Jim Marshall's Views from the Bridge

by James R. Marshall

Lake Superior Port Cities Inc.

First Edition: September 1999

LAKE SUPERIOR PORT CITIES INC.
P.O. Box 16417
Duluth, Minnesota 55816-0417
USA
888-BIG LAKE (244-5253) • www.lakesuperior.com

Publishers of *Lake Superior Magazine* and *Lake Superior Travel Guide*

Portions of this book have been previously published in *Lake Superior Magazine* and *Lake Superior Newsletter*

5 4 3 2 1

Marshall, James R.
    Lake Superior journal : Jim Marshall's views from the bridge /
    James R. Marshall
        p.   cm.
    Includes bibliographical references (p.) and index.
    ISBN 0-942235-40-1
    1. Superior, Lake – History Anecdotes. 2. Superior, Lake, Region – History Anecdotes. 3. Folklore – Superior, Lake. 4. Folklore – Superior, Lake, Region. 5. Superior, Lake Biography Anecdotes. 6. Superior, Lake, Region – Biography Anecdotes. I. Title.
    F552.M36   1999
    977.4'9 – dc21   99-41485
                                                                          CIP

Printed in the United States of America

    Editors: Paul L. Hayden, Hugh Bishop, Konnie LeMay
    Designer: Mathew Pawlak
    Printer: Cushing-Malloy Inc., Ann Arbor, Michigan

Dedicated to the Memory of
Stanley Sivertson,
Fisherman's Fisherman

Foreword

James R. Marshall is what many consider to be the consummate Lake Superior authority. He has done it all – prospector, scuba diver, shipwreck salvager, boat captain, airplane pilot, explorer, researcher. He has traveled all over the lake, encountering thousands of people, all of whom have contributed to his knowledge of the lake. His trips onto Lake Superior on *Skipper Sam* and *Skipper Sam II* have taken him to places we might only wish we could visit. He's brought it all to life through his bimonthly column "Lake Superior Journal" within the pages of *Lake Superior Magazine*. It is the most popular column in the magazine, and it deserves to be, because he tells a good tale.

From an editor's perspective, Jim Marshall is one of those hard writers to edit. He tells, and writes, a good story. And writers like this are the toughest kind for editors who are constantly trying to fit material into small spaces within a magazine. He weaves his stories in such a way that there's little superfluous material. You get entranced with his tale. One thought leads to the next and then to the next, and before you know it you're hooked with this bit of information about Lake Superior that makes your day a little better. We generally end up giving the story more space, not less.

Jim's wide range of interests blends perfectly with those of a regional magazine, allowing him to tell stories about all of the things that he finds interesting around the lake. His sizable personal library of early volumes about the region lends authority and depth to his work. From people to glaciers to shipwrecks and historical lore, this collection of his earliest writings offers a fascinating opportunity to explore Lake Superior from the comfort of an easy chair, while engaging you in Jim's "you are there" style of storytelling.

I have a bit of first-hand knowledge of the stories of Mr. Marshall. First of all, because he's my father-in-law, I've been privy to years of stories almost too numerous to count. JR, as he's known to his friends, has also been telling his tales of Lake Superior in his column for close to two decades. Like all good columns, it has won numerous writing awards. But best of all, it is liked by the readers.

Good stories deserve many retellings, and thus we present this first collection from the early years of the "Journal." We've given a sampler of some of the poignant, insightful and entertaining stories that have appeared in the magazine. Whether you're reading them for the first time or finding them again, we're sure you'll enjoy the treasures of Jim Marshall's "Lake Superior Journal."

Paul L. Hayden
Editor

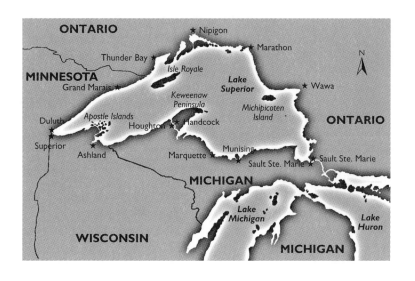

CONTENTS

Lake Superior Journal

The Mists of the Past

Among the Mysteries of Lake Superior

It's an eerie feeling, knowing with certainty that wherever we might picnic, hike or explore around our beautiful Lake Superior, we are not the first people to do so.

Ancient visitors probably regarded the same view and pondered similar thoughts thousands of years ago. I cannot tell you what they wore, where they came from or why they left the Lake Superior country. I can tell you they were most assuredly here, in great numbers, perhaps as long ago as 4,500 years. Indians encountered by even the earliest explorers professed absolutely no knowledge of this early race.

Shrouded in the mists of time, they are a mystery worthy of the legendary Sherlock Holmes, and indeed his creator came to Silver Islet, just east of Thunder Bay, Ontario, below the Sibley Peninsula, in 1934. Sir Arthur Conan Doyle, a renowned psychic, attended a gathering of noted mediums hosted by Julian Cross, owner of the old mining location and a fellow psychic. As later described by author Helen Moore Strickland, "clear communication was established with these early visitors, who spoke of the 'red metal' (copper)."

Our mystery race, now known as the Copper Culture, left incontrovertible evidence. Mining pits, literally thousands of them, dot Isle Royale and the Keweenaw Peninsula. The late professor Roy W. Drier of Calumet, Michigan, excavated a few pits in the McCargoe Cove area of Isle Royale in 1953 and 1955.

1

The Pukaskwa Pits of Ontario have intrigued scholars for centuries. Theories of Dr. Greg Bambenek (foreground) of Duluth, Minnesota, have placed them on a par with Stonehenge in significance to the early inhabitants of the Lake Superior region. The cobblestone pits could have been used to help predict fish spawning times. Sam Alvar photo.

Analysis of charred fragments found in the pits revealed them to be over 3,000 years old. His interest led to the publishing of the book *Prehistoric Copper Mining in the Lake Superior Region* with fellow scientist Octave Du Temple.

Truly mysterious are the famed Pukaskwa pits, found on the early beaches of the northeastern lakeshore. Again this evidence of early inhabitants is only now being measured and recorded.

Dr. Greg Bambenek of Duluth sees them as being like another Stonehenge, used by the ancients as an astronomical calendar. Bambenek feels these structures were used to predict spawning times, when fish could be taken in shallow water. A major food source, knowing when to fish would have been of great value to our early friends. These pits are in the pebble and cobblestone beaches of the lake, while the pits of Isle Royale and the south shore are found in solid rock.

There are so many of these pits in the bedrock that the early explorers and prospectors at first thought them to be natural. Only when each pit yielded "hammerstones," granite boulders showing chipped ends indicating use as a mining tool, did they realize they were looking at mining activity. One mining engineer described the pits as "the efforts of 10,000 men over 1,000 years."

Every pit excavated, and each adit (horizontal tunnel) examined, revealed the presence of a vein of native copper. An early theory described the building of fires on an exposed vein, heating the surrounding rock. Once the rock was hot, water would be poured on the surface, causing fractures and spalling. The hammerstones would then be used to expose and free the native copper.

In one pit, near Rockland, Michigan, Samuel Knapp, seeking a night's shelter in 1848, realized that the cave he had entered was not natural. Cleaning it out to a depth of 16 feet, he gradually exposed a piece of copper which had been freed from the host rock by the early miners. It was later found to weigh almost six tons. Several other pits yielded large masses, some partially elevated on rotting timbers. One must wonder just what the ancients intended to do with such unwieldy finds.

Another clue compounds the mystery. The hammerstones of the Keweenaw, so plentiful that our forebears used them for house foundations, almost always were grooved around their circumference. This probably enabled them to be tied to a sapling or handle, thus gaining leverage. Most of them are chipped on both ends, showing evidence of maximum use. The stones of Isle Royale, although plentiful, do not have this groove. They are usually chipped only on one end, indicating they were held in the hands of the miner.

Early explorers reaching the lake were told of a huge mass of copper located on a river. This five-ton mass, which became known as the Ontonagon Boulder, was displayed at the Smithsonian Institution in Washington, D.C. Considered holy by the Indians, it bears evidence of every bit of copper being removed wherever possible on its surface.

The pits are outlined in orange ribbon to help identify their pattern. Possible alignment of the pits with the sun aided early residents of the region in their survival. Sam Alvar photo.

Widespread publicity describing this find triggered the Lake Superior copper rush of 1846. By the mid-1800s, it was clear that every outcropping of copper had been mined once before by an ancient race, and that every modern copper mine was initially located by examination of ancient mining pits.

A most tantalizing clue has been advanced by students from Michigan Technological University in Houghton, Michigan. After extensive research, they theorized that the early mining might well have commenced when the lake was much higher, perhaps dammed at Sault Ste. Marie by the last receding glacier about 11,000 years ago. Creating a map based on elevations, they show that most of the pits would have been along the beaches of the lake during that period.

Our copper was used as trading material throughout the Americas, and possibly beyond. Specimens found on the beaches often exhibit specks and small masses of native silver combined with the copper.

When such a sample was sent to alchemists in France by the Jesuits, these early scientists concluded that the inhabitants of North America were far ahead of Europe in metallurgy. That silver and copper could be melted together, without becoming an alloy, was deemed (and is) impossible. To occur in nature was not even initially considered, but this is the case. Almost all Lake Superior copper contains some silver, and this is the method used today to trace copper artifacts, wherever found, back to our lake.

George W. "Rip" Rapp Jr. is a full professor of geology and archeology and Dean of the College of Science and Engineering at the University of Minnesota, Duluth. Since 1967, his travels in search of this link have taken him literally all over the world.

Others, such as Howard Scott of Ontonagon, Michigan, have devoted a lifetime to solving this mystery. His extensive writings reflect his deep commitment.

The Copper Culture is but one of the strange mysteries haunting our lake. Perhaps you have found examples of your own, those not-quite-explainable stories. We would like to hear of them and your questions. Please share them with us.

Originally appeared in Lake Superior Magazine, *July/August 1987*

In the Shadow of the Last Glacier

Jim Paquette is a no-nonsense guy, a hard-driving mechanical expert at his mining job, a sophisticated expert at his hobby of archaeology. With his wife, Karen, and his skilled partner, Dr. Marla Buckmaster of Northern Michigan University, he is part of a team whose work is revising accepted thought on early inhabitants of the Upper Peninsula.

For many years it was believed that the earliest inhabitants of the Lake Superior region were the copper seekers; the general time frame was 3,500 years B.P. This term, B.P., means "before present," as contrasted with the usual dating of B.C. or A.D. The academic community felt that no humans had visited what is now the south shore of Lake Superior much before the red metal that could be worked into tools was discovered.

Most of us have some understanding of the glaciers that covered the Great Lakes, advancing and receding over four major time periods across many thousands of years. The last major glacial period, known as the Wisconsin, had numerous arms of moving ice. The Terminal Moraine park and hiking trail system of Wisconsin outlines the final thrusts of this glacial age, with hundreds of gravel eskers, lakes and potholes marking movement and retreat of the ice.

In simplest form, glaciers are formed when climates generate more snow and cold weather than warm and melting conditions.

The glaciers of North America today have receded far to the north, but are still alive. Many are more than a mile thick, ice at the bottom being more than 10,000 years old. Some scientists feel we are living between ice ages, and they can supply evidence to support such a thesis.

While the approximately 3,000-year-old Copper Culture left abundant evidence of its presence, members have long been regarded as the first visitors to follow the glacial retreat. This conclusion has been challenged by people who, while lacking archaeological credentials, exude human curiosity. These folks, skilled in the outdoors and such professions as medicine, marketing and history, found much that caused them to wonder.

Jim Paquette screens material from units at the excavation site on the shore of Deer Lake in Ishpeming, Michigan. Many late Paleo-Indian artifacts have been discovered at this site. Jim Paquette photo.

We've reported on the strange Pukaskwa pits of northern Lake Superior, as described by Dr. Greg Bambenek. Others, like Catholic priests, whose travels brought them to Lake Superior almost 400 years ago, wrote of the early evidence: odd quartzite tools that were obviously the work of intelligent beings and hammered copper artifacts that filled an obvious early need. Many questions were raised, but none were answered.

The formal archaeological fraternity had long considered the Upper Peninsula of Michigan as a glacially scoured area, devoid of life or inhabitation prior to the Copper Culture of about 3,500 years ago. (B.P., if you are really into this!) Some fragmented reports of obvious prehistorical activity found little audience. If things didn't quite fit the agreed-upon time frames, they were usually overlooked. After all, the last glacier had left about 10,500 to 12,000 years B.P. (see, you are catching on) and this left a barren and inhospitable landscape.

"Who would want to live there?" was the question reinforcing the thinking of the time.

The Gribben Basin, south of Marquette, Michigan, became the site of a tailings basin for the Tilden Iron Mining Partnership. Exploring the ground as a requirement of their environmental

Jill Paquette holds an incredible ancient artifact, a large copper pike, found by her father near Teal Lake. Jim Paquette photo.

protection plan, workers found that a mature forest was entombed in the soil, some 60 feet below the current surface. Such a discovery triggered archaeological inquiry and exploration, resulting in a whole new look at the Upper Peninsula. With carbon-14 dating, the forest was found to be 10,000 years old.

In 1984, Jim Paquette was engaged in large equipment mechanical maintenance at the Tilden Mine. A magna cum laude graduate of Northern Michigan University, Jim had long been a student of history, and he sensed that the forest find was but one piece of the puzzle. If the climate at that time encouraged a forest to grow, he reasoned, wildlife must have been present.

Seeking food, early humans must have followed the animals into this forest. If they lived there, they must have left traces of their habitation, and Jim Paquette set out to find this evidence. He bought a metal detector.

The next question was where to look. He thought he might as well make it easy, at least to begin with. He set out for Teal Lake, immediately west of Negaunee, Michigan, and just a mile from home. At a site near the lake and in the shadow of a bold bluff, the metal detector reacted with enthusiasm. Copper artifacts were unearthed, some of striking beauty and in remarkably good condition.

Glancing over his shoulder, Jim realized that he was still near habitation. Fine homes were not far away. Packing the copper tools into his rucksack, he started for home.

"What," he wondered, "do I do with these?"

A telephone call arranged a visit with NMU archaeologist Dr. Marla Buckmaster. This contact initiated an ongoing team effort, with Buckmaster adding skilled professionalism as well as excitement to the unfolding drama.

Paquette's search continued, with Buckmaster confirming the location of a series of ancient campsites along the shoreline of Teal Lake in Negaunee. An analysis of the artifacts uncovered at these sites led researchers to conclude that prehistoric people once lived in the Negaunee area as long ago as 6000 B.C., several thousand years earlier than previous evidence had led archaeologists to believe.

This exciting revelation resulted in an intensified search by Buckmaster and Paquette to uncover additional evidence about the origins of early inhabitants in Michigan's Upper Peninsula.

Buckmaster and other scientists confirmed that Paquette had found evidence that Marquette County was once the home of truly ancient bands of Paleo and early Archaic Indians. These people had set foot on this land at the very time the great ice sheets were disappearing from the Lake Superior basin, some 10,000 years ago!

Michigan state archaeologist Dr. John Halsey says that Paquette's "work in identifying these important early interior sites represents one of the major developments in U.P. archaeology in the last 20 years."

Paquette's work has been reported in several scientific journals and he is joining Buckmaster in additional publication projects.

What has emerged from this research and exploration raises as many questions as it appears to answer. Imagine these stalwart hunters, dealing with all types of wildlife, who sought the lush grasses springing up on the glacial gravels. Were they a society, as Jim Paquette thinks they must have been? Were they here by the thousands, as his research seems to indicate?

He shared his conclusions and some of the mysteries still remaining in the December/January 1996 issue of *Lake Superior Magazine* and is still making finds at sites he has identified in his home territory.

Originally appeared in Lake Superior Magazine, *August/September 1993*

Diary of an 1846 Visit to Lake Superior

The autumn air was crisp, the view spectacular. Leaving Duluth, Minnesota, on Highway 23, I had stopped at the top of the hill just outside of Fond du Lac. This particular tourist viewpoint, one of several on the "Evergreen Memorial Highway," looks to the north. I've always thought of the land in view to be almost "bowl like" and uninhabited. Both Carlton and Cloquet can be visualized in the distance and the mighty St. Louis River borders the whole scene.

Another car, northbound, pulled in, breaking the reverie of the moment. Two adults and two travel-weary children alighted from the automobile and soon were peering over the embankment.

"Nothing here," was the incredulous remark. "Why would they waste money on a place to just look at woods?"

Motioning toward their car, the driver said, "Let's go find something worth looking at."

He glanced at me with a look of pity, like I must be a pretty dull fool to be there at all, or I'm awfully short of better things to do.

Keeping my mouth shut is, according to my friends, not my longest suit. I considered a remark and decided against saying anything.

The young lad looked at me with obvious curiosity. "What are you looking at, mister?"

"This country is your travel route today," I said, with a sweep of my arm, "but people have traveled this country for thousands of years, usually by canoe and packsack."

His gaze followed my gesture; he raised his eyes to examine the whole scene. "First Indians, then early explorers used this same route as they sought the far country," I said.

It was clear I had sparked his interest, but his father called him. They drove away, discussing, no doubt, the eccentric character they had just seen.

One early tourist didn't just move on. He was totally taken with the incredible beauty of the country. And he recorded his impressions in 1846, almost a century and a half ago!

His book, published in New York in 1847 and titled *Summer In The Wilderness*, was based upon extensive diaries. Beginning in St. Louis, Missouri, Charles Lanman ascended the Mississippi River to its source, noting carefully the country and its inhabitants. He crossed to the St. Louis River in Minnesota by means of the Savanna Portage, easily the worst portage ever used by early visitors. Wading in swamps and mud, he and his party fought mosquitoes, soaked clothing and fatigue, finally arriving on the banks of the St. Louis River near what we now know as Floodwood, Minnesota.

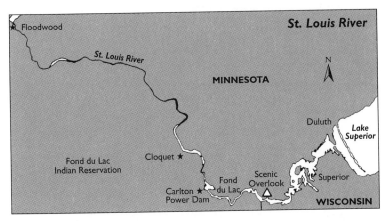

In so doing, he became one of the first Europeans to negotiate the rugged terrain of Knife Falls, the area now well known as Jay Cooke State Park. Located just west of Duluth, the swift water and upright slates evoke fear and wonder in any traveler pausing to enjoy the sight.

Lanman was obviously well-bred and financially comfortable. He saw beauty in what others called a miserable wilderness and found friends among the Ojibway nation as he traveled.

Writing one of the many letters he used to later create his wonderful little book, Lanman notes he is at the "Mouth of the Saint Louis, August 1846. By looking at the map you will observe that this river enters Lake Superior on the extreme west. I had not the means of ascertaining its precise length, but was told that above the Savannah, where I struck it, it is an inconsiderable stream."

In our day, the highways we travel cross rivers frequently. We seldom even notice. To the early traveler, moving water often meant death or hardship. And it was treated with respect. Simultaneously, the early pioneer appreciated the relief that floating baggage gave from the dangerous and difficult trail.

Lanman's description of the St. Louis River continues: "From that point to the lake it is quite a majestic river, and I should suppose the distance to be nearly 150 miles. It has more the appearance of a wild New England river than any other that I have seen in the western country. It is exceedingly rocky, and so full of sunken boulders and dangerous rapids that it never could be made navigable further up than Fond du Lac, which is 20 miles from Lake Superior."

Lanman describes the clear but "snuff colored" water, the lack of habitation except for the trading post (at Fond du Lac) and the rapid change in water level. "But," he adds, "I hear the roar of its glorious cataracts and must attempt a description of them.

"There is a place on this river," he says, "called the Knife Portage, from the fact the rocks here are exceedingly sharp and pointed, where the stream forms a large bend, and where the voyageur has to make a portage of 12 miles. The length of this bend may be 16 miles, and in that distance the water has a fall of about 320 feet.

"The width of the river may be from three to four hundred yards. At this point (just above Fond du Lac) are three nameless waterfalls, whose dimensions are indeed stupendous; they are said to be the largest in the Northwest. The water of the first tumbles over a pile of pointed rocks, and after twisting itself into every possible variety of schutes and foaming streams, finally murmurs itself to sleep in a pool 80 feet below the summit whence it takes its first step.

"The second fall, or rather cataract, is about 140 feet high, nearly perpendicular and the water rushes over in a solid and almost unbroken body."

It is obvious that Lanman is taken with the beauty of this enchanted place, as he describes the lofty walls of slate "crowned with a peculiar diadem of trees; and as the roaring of the fall is perfectly deafening, its effect upon me was allied to that of Niagara." He describes the pools "black and fathomless, with spray whiter than snow."

Lanman had traveled countless miles with his Chippewa companions, and the larger group he was a part of was en route to La Pointe, Wisconsin, on Madeline Island, for treaty payment. He was covering country not previously known to "white people from the States" and he did not treat the honor lightly.

The third and final rapids was some two miles below Knife Falls, covered today, I believe, by a power dam. "The next

12

perpendicular fall, within the bend I have mentioned, is some two miles downstream, and is only about 50 feet in height, but its grandeur is enhanced by the rapids which succeed it."

His respect for his companions shows in his remarks. "An old trader tells me I am the first traveller from the states who has ever taken the trouble actually to visit these cataracts. If this is a fact, as the Indians, so far as I can learn, have never christened them, I claim the privilege of giving them a name. Let them, then, be known hereafter as the Chippeway Falls."

And, these many years later, so shall they remain.

Originally appeared in Lake Superior Magazine, *August/September 1991*

Chequamegon Bay – The Early Years

His name was Benjamin G. Armstrong. He came to Wisconsin in the early 1830s and over the next 60 years took part in the making of the territory and the development of what we now call Chequamegon Bay, the Apostle Islands Country.

Benjamin Armstrong knew the Chippewa well, gaining their trust and giving them council as they struggled to comprehend the meaning of the treaties being offered them by the "Great White Father."

With almost no resources, he accompanied the great Chief Buffalo to Washington, D.C., acting as a spokesman for the Chippewa in this totally foreign scene. The treaties, most especially the 1854 agreement signed at La Pointe on Madeline Island in the Apostles, is still being debated. This is where the controversial fishing rights were granted which inflame passions around Lake Superior to this day.

Try as he might, Armstrong could not convey to the U.S. government the basic flaw in its proposals. The intent of the United States was to acquire the land under any terms that would allow safe access by white men. They could not comprehend that the Ojibway nation did not think of itself as "owners" of the lands they occupied.

Time and time again, our government signed solemn treaties, made sincere commitments and promised certain types of compensation. It was Benjamin Armstrong who often "held their feet to the fire" encouraging fulfillment. He made many enemies.

In 1890, with the help of Thomas P. Wentworth, Armstrong published his memoirs in a book *Early Life Among the Indians*. I am privileged to own a copy, printed by the "Press of A.W. Bowron, Ashland, Wisconsin, 1892."

Though not at all a well-known work, it is a fascinating historical glimpse of life and adventure in the northern part of Wisconsin.

Many subjects are covered, from the mystery of the mound builders to an unabashed appraisal of Father Frederic Baraga.

Speaking of the famous "Snowshoe Priest" of Lake Superior,

Armstrong says: "Father Baraga was probably the best posted man in the Chippewa language who ever attempted to explain it and write up their customs and religious beliefs, but he fell in error. I had frequent talks with him about his works, and he explained them to me as he understood them and gave the source of the greater part of his information. I did not tell him the source of my information and never attempted to disabuse his mind of the error. The facts are that the source from which my information was derived was the head of the Chippewa church, while his was obtained from the foot of it."

"Don't Eat Moose Until You Catch Him" is the caption under this woodcut which appears in Early Life Among the Indians.

In this simple passage, and in subsequent paragraphs, Benjamin Armstrong states his respect for the priest and in the process explains – to a degree – the beauty of the Chippewa faith.

To hundreds of sailboaters, Hermit Island in the Apostles holds the "air of mystery" often associated with lost treasure, foul play and murder. Armstrong recounts knowing a man named Wilson who lived on the island in the 1850s. A strange and lonely man, he lived the life of a hermit, making barrels for the fish companies.

Wilson came to Armstrong's home on nearby Oak Island to get the barrel of whisky he had asked Armstrong to order for him.

Wilson then asked Armstrong to accompany him back to his island to help him unload the barrel, saying he would pay

Armstrong for the whisky and then bring him back to Oak Island. Again, in Armstrong's words:

"He brought out either three or four bags of coin in buckskin and one stocking-leg filled with coin and laid them on the table. From one he counted out the money for me, and when he had finished asked, 'Is that enough?' I told him it was and a little too much and gave him back some change...."

Armstrong goes on to recount how Wilson sensed him to be honest and asked him to count all his money for him. The amount totaled almost $1,300, a fortune for that time and place.

In 1861, Armstrong learned no smoke had been seen coming from Wilson's chimney for several days. He went to La Pointe and informed Judge Bell of the unusual circumstance. Bell said that he had not seen the Hermit for two months and would gather some men to go out there with Armstrong and check.

They found Wilson dead on the floor of his cabin, and "appearances indicated that he had been murdered."

Armstrong then explained to the judge what had transpired some years before. A thorough search of the house and area was instituted, yielding only $60 found behind the clock and "entirely hidden from sight when the clock was in place."

One can only conclude several searches followed, but no record of the money being found has ever surfaced.

This fellow Bell was the famous (and, to some, infamous) "King of the Apostle Islands," whom Armstrong describes and explains in remarkably unbiased terms. An example of the way Bell ran La Pointe is contained in the story of a man named Wright who had the misfortune to find himself involved in "interference of the law" while awaiting a boat at La Pointe.

Judge Bell as Sheriff issued a complaint to himself as Judge, issued the necessary warrant, which he himself then served, bringing the prisoner before his own tribunal, where he sentenced him to pay a fine of $400 or serve six months in jail. Wright would not pay the fine, and "the Judge put him in jail, but it was not properly provided with locks, and the prisoner escaped."

Learning that the prisoner had escaped to Douglas County, Bell journeyed there, took him prisoner again and returned him to La Pointe.

Though the jail now had been equipped with locks, the hole in the roof for the stove chimney offered another avenue of escape, and Wright had boarded a boat when the Judge learned of his departure.

Again Bell seized his man, who had by this time explained his plight to a traveling lawyer aboard the boat.

Being unaware of Bell's total role, the new attorney informed the fellow that he assumed to be just a law officer that Wright had been unlawfully returned from Douglas County and thus should not be held.

Straightening to his full height, the visiting lawyer said, "You cannot go into another county and take a man on your own warrant."

Judge Bell listened and then replied, "Can't, eh! But I did, and the man is now in my jurisdiction and will take the consequences of my sentence, which I now reaffirm."

(Exit lawyer just in time to catch the boat.)

Sounds like just traveling through La Pointe in the mid-1800s was almost as dangerous as hunting bear with your bare hands.

Originally appeared in Lake Superior Magazine, *December/January 1989*

Protecting the Treasures of Canoe Rocks

Skipper Sam II cleared Blake Point, the rugged northeast end of Isle Royale, bound for Thunder Bay, Ontario. The fabled Sleeping Giant, the awesome mass of Sibley Peninsula marking the eastern approach to Thunder Bay, seemed much closer than the 26 miles I knew it to be.

To the southwest, the shimmering loveliness of giant Pie Island marked the other pillar of the entrance. The lake was flat, the sky azure with just a few cottony cumulus clouds. Camera in hand, crew member Dave Poirier waved his arm across the broad vista, gesturing in frustration.

"Where," he asked, "should I aim to capture even a fraction of all this?"

He is right. On such a day, camera film later reflects tiny segments of an overwhelming view well known to those who traverse the expanse of northern Lake Superior.

First mate Jan appeared on the bridge, a tray of coffee and assorted calories in hand. Shading her eyes with a downturned palm, she pointed at the tiny dots of Canoe Rocks, some four miles to the northwest.

"Is this the day," she asked, "to visit the graves of the *Emperor* and the *Congdon?*"

The question was fair. This leg of open lake, from Blake Point to the sometimes dubious shelter of Thunder Bay, is not always amenable to sightseeing. In fact, some boaters can exhibit indentations in their teak or mahogany trim that bear the faint traces of fingerprints!

The channel between Isle Royale and the north shore is open for almost 200 miles to the southwest and more than 100 miles to the northeast. Wind of any consequence could disturb the tranquility we were experiencing on this day of days.

Canoe Rocks beckoned. Nudging the throttles, our Chrysler helpmates responded with the enthusiasm of well-trained Siberian huskies getting a glimpse of the trail.

Soon we were right next to these wave-worn sentinels, engines stopped, staring in amazement down into the clear water. Just a shadowy visage was discernible, the ice-crushed pilothouse of the *Emperor*. Mooring buoys, placed here for the charter diving boats, looked for all the world like tethered balloons in the clear water.

In response to the questioning looks of the crew, we discussed the *Emperor's* fatal error in the early morning of June 4, 1947. Laden with iron ore, the 525-foot vessel had left Port Arthur in thick fog, en route to Ashtabula, Ohio. A serious navigation error put her on Canoe Rocks with such force that she broke in two and sank almost immediately. Eleven crew members and her captain, Eldon Walkinshaw, went down with her to their deaths.

Inside the cabin of the Emperor, *a nesting bunk bed still clings to the wall. The Emperor sank at Canoe Rocks near Isle Royale in 1947. Elmer Engman photo.*

Response to her SOS came almost immediately from the U.S. Coast Guard cutter *Kimball*, which was in the area servicing navigational aids. She arrived at the site in just 25 minutes, picking up seven survivors from the rocks themselves and 14 more from two lifeboats.

The *Emperor* is a mecca for scuba divers, encouraged to just look her over and preserve her for others to inspect. This was not always the case. In past years the old ship and the reef that sank her have seen some of the more bizarre Lake Superior diving adventures.

One cast of characters from Taconite Harbor, Minnesota, came to the conclusion that the *Emperor's* propeller was made of solid

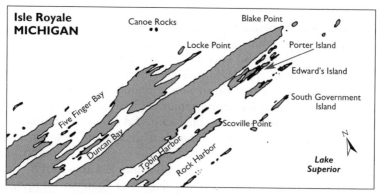

brass. The value of such a mass would be significant, and so a plan was devised whereby it would be removed and converted to green paper spending units.

A whole batch of plans was hatched to remove the giant casting from its shaft. The prospect of several tons of metal loose in better than 150 feet of water, either dangerously buoyant or one heck of a big anchor for a small boat, gave pause to the enthusiasm. Finally, a combination of weather, inadequate boats and other obstructions caused the effort to lose its appeal and die a natural death.

Only in later years was a close inspection made of the propeller – it wasn't brass at all!

Through all those early visits, more and more divers began to report the presence of a body in the after end of the ship, in more than 125 feet of water. It was there, all right. And finally some well-meaning gentlemen decided it should be returned to the surface for proper burial. The theory was adequate, but the remains were less than enthusiastic about changing their eternal resting place. Without excess detail harming everyone's lunch, it became a rather messy undertaking.

In earlier years, the upper portion of the pilothouse had been crushed by ice action, but clear access was available to the main deck level of the forward cabin, where countless five-gallon pails of "red lead" were stored.

Twenty years ago such treasure meant value to some of the divers, and pilferage continued until rust made lifting the pails dangerous. Many were the wet suits bearing dirty reddish brown smudges – usually proof of a visit to the shallow end of the *Emperor*.

In the 1960s, a crew of divers from Milwaukee arrived at the site in a beat-up old boat. Not long after, a small safe appeared in the shallow water just south of Belle Isle dock, about five miles

20

from the wreck site. Covered with rust, its door had been pried open, and it was empty.

The same crew showed up the next season, this time in a fancy craft that attracted the attention of the Park Service. After they were observed trying to scavenge another wreck, they were asked to vacate the park, permanently. Wreck pilferage is rare today, but it wasn't always this way.

The storytelling concluded with the arrival of the *Royale Diver*, an Isle Royale diving charter boat. We watched as another group prepared to visit the wreck, backing away as they raised the white striped red "diver below" flag.

There was time for just a momentary pause above the *Congdon*, a November 6, 1918, victim of these same shoals.

With an exchange of friendly waves, we resumed our passage to Thunder Bay, the lake still flat.

Originally appeared in Lake Superior Magazine, *August/September 1990*

CHAPTER TWO

Treasure Hunters of the Lake

The Johns Family of Isle Royale

Snug as you are in your possibly snowbound castle, let me challenge your imagination for a moment. Let your mind transport you to Washington Harbor, Isle Royale, Michigan, locked as it still is in winter's icy grip. Almost without thought you pull the hood of your parka closer about your face, even though you are sheltered by a cluster of balsams just up the hill from the ice-encrusted dock.

Through the swirling snow the tiny cabin is barely visible, shuttered tightly against the encroaching storm. No welcoming light is visible, as it once was; no one tends a warming fire. You are here alone on Johns Island. You are very alone.

The roar of that first cannon shot of the Civil War was yet to be heard by those at Fort Sumter when settlers arrived at this tiny island. Captain John F. Johns and his wife, Catherine, tiring of the copper country mines, sought a better life in this sheltered harbor. True Cornish mining people, they had come to Houghton, Michigan, responding to the promise of cheap land and good wages that had lured so many of their brethren.

In the strictest of definitions, the promise was true. There was land, almost for the taking, but the long days underground in the mine, plus the high cost of food and supplies at the company store, limited progress. They had heard of the island out in the lake and decided to seek their fortune and future there.

Their first activity at Isle Royale was commercial fishing, but it was not long

The Johns family built the first hotel on Isle Royale in the early 1900s. This picture was taken prior to 1916. Johns Family Collection.

before Capt. Johns was contacted by the mining men of the Isle Royale Land Corporation. An unusual organization, the company was restricted by its charter to land development and exploration only; even though the men might find copper, they were not to mine it. They wanted Johns to assist them in prospecting.

He had acquired his mining experience and the title of mine captain across the Atlantic in Cornwall; his work in the Michigan mines further enhanced his reputation. He participated in the exploration of the north side of the island, which culminated in the location of rich copper at McCargoe Cove. Another company, originally known as the Minong Mining Company, developed this mine, and Capt. Johns worked for this firm for several years.

During this period several children were born to the family, two of whom, Capt. William and Capt. John Johns, went on to become ship captains. They owned and operated the steamer *Crescent* between Duluth, Minnesota, and Port Arthur, Ontario, from 1912 to 1918. A third son, Edgar, worked with his father as they homesteaded and thus gained title to three islands in Washington Harbor, now known as Johns, Barnum and Laura (also known as Salt Island). Edgar also owned Thompson Island in later years.

The whole family worked at fishing and mining, taking an active part in the last mining activity on the island. In 1890, the Wendigo (spelled with an "e") Copper Company built a town in Washington Harbor to support the development of their mine nearby. Known as Ghyllbank, the settlement was located where the present Windigo Ranger Station now stands. Capt. Johns was involved in construction at the townsite and at the mine.

Bob Johns on the foredeck of the Cox where, he recalls, "You could feel slight motion of the ship." Note the horizon line. Johns Family Collection.

Unfortunately, the mine treated the developers better than the stockholders, and little copper was produced.

The family built the first hotel on Isle Royale, a large portion of which still stands on Barnum Island. They operated the first post office, in conjunction with their commercial fishing operations.

With the demise of mining, the family enlarged their fishing operations, which continued into the 1920s. Edgar married the granddaughter of a legendary mining man, Capt. William Jacka, who had run the Minong Copper Mine, easily the most successful mine on the island. Edgar worked for George Barnum of Duluth in several capacities, spending many summers at the island the Barnums had purchased from the Johns family as well as on the Johns family island just across the harbor. His son, Robert, was born in 1916 and grew up on Isle Royale. Bob went on to a career in banking in Duluth, but still returns to the island with his family each summer. He has a deep love for the lake and his island, as well as numerous stories about his 71 years of visits.

The stranding of the *George M. Cox* was certainly one of Bob's more exciting experiences. The *Cox* was rounding the southwest end of Isle Royale in 1933, running fast in a low, dense fog. The keeper of Rock of Ages light could see the tops of her masts as she rushed toward the reef just south of the lighthouse, apparently unaware of the fog signal he was sounding. The photographs tell the rest of the story.

24

The *Cox* was not salvaged, breaking in two in October of that year and settling on the bottom of the lake where she remains today.

Earlier, in 1925, Bob and his family were literally marooned on Isle Royale into December, far past the usual time of winter departure. The steamer *America*, the lifeline of transportation for all the island families, had struck a reef near the island and was in dry dock in Port Arthur for repairs. As Bob remembers, the cold was intense, and the little food remaining consisted of herring, bread and honey. Days dragged by, occupied by the constant search for more and more firewood.

It was December 4th before the *America's* welcome whistle was finally heard. In excited haste the family rowed their loaded skiff across the harbor to Booth's dock on Booth Island, where the *America* would tie up. Coming alongside the structure, a giant wave lifted them high above and over the dock, finally depositing them in upright safety as it receded. They left the skiff there for the winter – overturned and lashed to the dock – and boarded the ship.

The crew of the *America* had to cut firewood on Booth Island to make sure they would have enough steam for the rough trip to Duluth. Many of the passengers helped haul the fuel, and the ship finally started out.

The lake was in the grip of a violent winter storm, making the passage extremely difficult.

The crew of Rock of Ages lighthouse, which marks the southwest end of Isle Royale, told quite a story the following spring. From their vantage point, they recalled, the *America* actually disappeared between waves as it left the island on that December day.

As Bob Johns well remembers, the *America* was 180 feet long!

Originally appeared in Lake Superior Magazine, *April/May 1988*

Duluth's Birch Tree Boys

Not all of Lake Superior treasure hunters muck around for mineral wealth. A few years ago, two of Duluth's high profile fellows attempted to tap the treasure trove in less strenuous fashion.

Having survived the boom and bust cycles of timber, iron ore, meat packing and shipbuilding, the lovely birch tree has enabled Duluth, Minnesota, the Zenith City of the Unsalted Seas, to stand now at the portal of unparalleled prosperity!

No, my friends, not another government boondoggle of tainted funds extracted from suffering taxpayers. Duluth's new stream of revenue comes from that capital of sound financial stability – Hollywood.

You see, we have something that the southern California community, of both unstable tectonic plates and marital relationships, lacks. We have birch trees.

It seems every screenwriter likes to film at least one scene in a setting resplendent with glistening birch. Real white birch doesn't exist, or is a rare commodity, on the West Coast.

This story stars John Goldfine, a somewhat unconventional local businessman and all-around character, and Rory Strange, late of the Duluth Convention and Visitors Bureau and at the time of this story associated with the marketing of the Duluth State Convention Center being nestled into the Arena-Auditorium complex.

A handsome, impeccably dressed executive, Rory's first real fame came when a Canadian lock keeper on the St. Lawrence Seaway aborted his attempt to bring a real live whale to Duluth.

Okay, with the elements of this tale now largely in place, let's go back to last fall and the filming, in Duluth, of "Far North," a Sam Sheppard/Jessica Lange extravaganza. They needed a soundproof stage area, and Rory dragged them through just about every industrial site in Duluth. The large building on the Port Terminal was most appealing, but concern was expressed about just how much noise Lake Superior's famous rain storms might make on the roof.

"Not to worry," piped the ever-optimistic Rory and within 10 minutes a large contingent of the Duluth Fire Department had giant nozzles spraying a torrent on the building. It could not be heard inside, and work proceeded apace, with Sheppard making a mental note of the tidal wave cascading from the building.

"A fine spot to do 'Noah's Ark,'" he observed.

When a small blonde girl was needed for a part in the movie, a line of parents several blocks long formed almost instantly, each having in tow a small blonde girl. The director was fascinated, admitting such positive interest from a community is quite rare.

Others in the cast discovered the Pickwick Restaurant and the Minnesota Surplus Store, where clothing for frontier survival abounded.

John Goldfine observed something else. Namely, his several family businesses, mostly hotels, shared in the new money brought by the cast and supporting crews involved in the production.

Confiding this new-found knowledge to Rory, they concluded Hollywood just needed a little old-fashioned selling, and Duluth would be awash in movie production. The buzz words had been noted by Rory: Duluth is "on the frontier," has "real birch trees" and "a whole bunch of nice people," according to the Hollywood visitors.

The thought incubated as fall turned to winter and, as the snow deepened, the two joined the rest of the population in dreaming of warm and sunny places. Canny folks, they realized that their employers were unlikely to spring for a cruise or a couple of weeks in the Virgin Islands, but perhaps a sales trip to that smog-bound film capital could be sold.

"It would be a tough, dirty assignment," Rory observed.

"Someone has to do it," John responded.

Adopting thin-lipped grimaces, they announced their acceptance of this self-created task to their associates. Trudging through the airport, wearing a properly downcast mien common to those being led to the death row section of a prison, they curried the sympathies of the lucky ones whose only exposure to hardship was seeing them off.

Only now has the rest of this tale come to light.

Arriving in Los Angeles, an almost magical transformation took place as the two realized the magnitude of their responsibility. Ever mindful of the need to conserve their limited funds, it was decided to rent an older car so as not to look like the "city slickers" who usually come to Hollywood. They found just the machine – a fully restored 1952 Ford convertible.

John, who eschews stockings in any form, complemented his bib-overalls with an outlandish Hawaiian shirt, designed to distract the viewer's attention from his mukluks.

Rory, who does bear some passing resemblance to Arne, the divorce lawyer on "L.A. Law," slid into a suit, white shirt and tie and then behind the wheel. Off they went, top down, hair flying, the subject of amazed stares from other motorists.

Rory Strange (left) and John Goldfine bedecked themselves in Hollywood style to sell the merits of Duluth to movie makers. Lake Superior Magazine *photo.*

Phone book and city map in hand, they began making calls. Pulling up to a studio gate, Rory would wave grandly to the dumfounded gate security as John would accelerate the car by putting his foot on Rory's shined Oxford.

The word quickly spread, and very important people began making room in their schedules for this pair of characters from the "frontier."

The Far North crew had spread Duluth's fame across Hollywood.

"Cripes, have we got birch trees," John would begin, waving his arms in a rather grand flourish."

"Lots of real friendly people and a surplus store right on the main street," Rory would add, radiating a smile.

"And we're right on the FRONTIER, with real woods just over the hill," they would exclaim in unison.

As they got into the spirit, this third statement was usually accompanied by a little impromptu dance, followed by a bow and the snapping of John's overall straps.

"Come make your movies in Duluth," was the message.

And why not?

Originally appeared in Lake Superior Magazine, *May/June 1988*

The Susies: Lake Superior's Treasure Islands

This is haunted, lonely and sacred ground. It has heard the laughter of prehistoric children running on the peculiar "rocks that ring," which fascinate the occasional modern visitor. Just walking on these abundant light gray beaches generates a unique bell-like sound.

Nestled into the north shore of Lake Superior some 38 miles northeast of Grand Marais, Minnesota, the Susie Islands lie just south of the Canadian border, near Pigeon Point. Most of the islands bear feminine names, honoring the daughters of an early resident family, the Falconers.

While the land immediately to the north and west forms a protective shield, it also carries the highway, with its vantage points. Travelers approaching the border crossing are offered a spectacular view of the Susies, and many accept that gift.

The motor vessel *Wenonah*, flagship of the Sivertson Grand Portage-Isle Royale Transportation Line, offers a splendid visit to these remote islands. The *Wenonah* leaves the stockade dock at Grand Portage at 9 a.m. each summer morning for its daily trip to Isle Royale. Once commanded by Captain Stanley Sivertson himself, the first pause of the voyage is at the famous Witch Tree. Growing out of solid rock with no soil evident, the legendary "spirit little cedar tree" of the Ojibway people is found on the north side of Hat Point, which divides Grand Portage Bay and Wauswaugoning Bay. Here the voyageurs celebrated the completion of their long traverse from Montreal by throwing their hats high in the air.

Crossing Wauswaugoning Bay, the vessel winds its way through the Susies before setting a resolute course for Isle Royale. The crew will explain the islands in detail. With but a moment's study, the several beaches of a much earlier Lake Superior are clearly discerned, formed of the softer slate boulders and pebbles between the rhyolite and diabase flows.

Susie Island itself is one of the larger islands and was several times the target of mining activity as early as the 1860s. Now covered with deadfalls and other unmistakable signs of an overly mature forest, it once was the site of a copper mining operation led by Ebenezer Falconer, who brought in machinery and equipment around 1912.

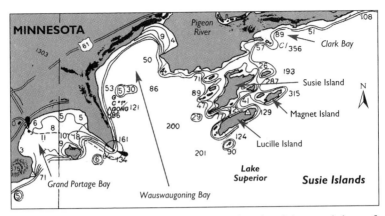

The Falconer family lived on the north side of the north bay of Susie Island and engaged in fishing for a livelihood. All had explored the old shaft on the southeast side of the island, where the Boston and Silver Islet Mining Company had mined in the 1870s in their constant search for additional veins. The shaft had been developed further by others after 1870, but by 1900 it was just another water-filled monument to the adage "more money has been put into the ground than has ever been removed."

The south side of Susie belongs to the Nature Conservancy, acquired to protect several rare plant species that have been found there. The old mine is on the north side, and we looked in earnest for its location some years ago.

Following the interface of slate and native rock, we climbed higher and higher, suddenly coming upon a man-made rock pile. It was an unmistakable sign of a mine, and within minutes we turned up the water-filled shaft.

My thoughts turned back a dozen years, focusing on the vivid memory of a 92-year-old man, a veteran of Isle Royale's mining years. The crackly voice of old Captain Edgar Johns described a suddenly missing mining partner who, he said, had met with foul play "and lies at the bottom of the shaft!" In disjointed fragments of recall, the old mining captain alluded darkly to the man "messing with a lady," which led at least to his disappearance, if not his untimely demise.

The shaft had descended at least 100 feet, at a rather sharp angle, as the vein of copper was followed, and a goodly amount of "stamp rock," chunks of rock containing mostly bits and pieces of copper, had been hand picked from the rock sent to the surface.

Starting below the mine tailings pile, a dock structure had been built in the lake, reaching across the shallow boulder-covered shelf

31

to the deep water portion of the north bay. Barrels of copper, the reward for a year of labor in the young mine, were rolled out to the end of the dock.

When the boat came, it would pause for only a moment to load, and the workers would have to be ready. Though the bay was wide open to the northeast, it was felt that the strong dock, weighted down with copper rock, could survive any blow.

As fall approached, word was sent to Grand Marais by way of a fisherman that a valuable cargo of copper awaited pickup at Susie Island. "Have the steamer *America* stop," was the instruction, and each passing day was framed with increasing concern as no boat came near the island.

Ebenezer Falconer was distraught. Somehow the message had not gotten out, so it was up to the miner to row to Grand Marais himself and pass the message of now pressing need. In a small rowboat, he dipped his oars with a sense of great urgency.

The trip took five days, two of which were spent in Horseshoe Bay at Hovland hiding from a terrible northeaster. In Grand Marais, Ebenezer boarded the *America* for the trip back to Susie, making small talk with the mate as they approached the bay.

Rounding the east side of Susie Island, Ebenezer stared in disbelief at the now calm bay. No trace of the long dock he had labored to build, or of the many barrels of copper, was evident. As the *America* paused, the Falconer children rowed out to get their father.

Tears were evident on all the small faces.

"The storm took everything," they cried. "Everything."

Settling himself in the boat for the trip to shore, Falconer reviewed all that had transpired since they had settled here after the arduous trip from their Scandinavian homeland.

"Children," he sternly addressed them, "no more tears. Help me count all we have left, not what we have lost...."

In but a few moments, laughter prevailed as the little boat nudged the shore.

Originally appeared in Lake Superior Magazine, *April/May 1990*

Not ALL that Glitters Is ...

Yessiree! Real honest-to-goodness Spanish treasure, just waiting there to be scooped up from the warm shallow waters of the Gulf of Mexico, the Bahamas and the Caribbean. Why, this is the opportunity of a LIFETIME!

A boiler room salesman? A smooth-talking, well-dressed stranger – with a diamond stickpin? Not on your tintype, my suspicious reader; this exclamation came from a good friend, a well known diver with treasure hunting credentials. Having been a diver myself, with a longtime interest in its rewards, I snagged a fingernail reaching for my checkbook.

The pitch was deceptively understated. Mel Fisher, the Key West treasure hunter who had found the *Senora de Atocha* treasure galleon, with its $400 million in treasure, had disbanded his group.

One of the most skilled members was beginning a new venture, to be called Underwater Action Adventures Incorporated. The idea was to sell weeks of treasure searching to the scuba-diving fraternity across America, for a nominal fee. Anyone buying in would get a share of anything found. A limited number of shares were available in the founding organization. But, I was told, I had to act QUICKLY! A bank money order wasn't fast enough; the money had to be wired immediately.

The ground floor, it seemed, was not too roomy on this particular castle in the clouds and I hustled to the local Western Union office.

A shiny new Cadillac on the avenue evoked a sneer. "I'll take that color, I noted, but in a Lincoln."

The urgency must have been alleviated by my infusion of capital because I didn't hear anything more from either my friend or UAAI. Winter beget spring, which turned to summer, and, during our vacation, who should I run into on the Bayfield, Wisconsin, dock but my treasure-hunting acquaintance.

He was dumfounded to learn that I was not up to date on the activities of UAAI, which was on the verge, he excitedly told me, of buying the largest commercial flower greenhouse in Florida. "Every bank and office in America needs green plants, and this is going to

33

be the source of an unending stream of dollars."

He didn't seem too sure of just what had happened to the flocks of divers, who I had thought were flailing the water to a froth, while paying for the privilege of finding truckloads of gold for me. He mumbled something about the FCC holding things up. What, I asked, did the Federal Communications Commission have to do with my gold-digging friends?

"Well," he said, "it's one of those darned guvamint outfits, maybe the FAA."

Federal Aviation Agency?

"Are we buying aircraft with our money?" I asked. The questions, I realized, just didn't fit the Bayfield dock in the summertime. I didn't extend our dialogue to the Securities and Exchange Commission, but I thought he was trying to remember the SEC. I just knew that Roger Hartley, Vlasie Solon and a few more of those Duluth stockbrokers would want to know more about this selling of plants to banks because I'd seen them go into banks, more than once. So I asked for a current address for UAAI, which somehow my friend had misplaced.

"I'll mail it to you," he promised.

Time passed and another winter was upon us. I assumed the greenhouse business must have been good because they didn't ask for more money or explain how business was going. I asked my friendly financial advisor about the source of the greenery in his bank.

"Some lady cleans it once in a while," he said. "It's plastic."

A letter arrived. It explained that the greenhouse idea had been a passing thought, searching for gold was not the "in thing" just now, but, if I would just sign the enclosed proxy, I would need a bigger mailbox to handle all the checks in no time.

Great Golconda Mineral Processors was the target, a Colorado-based firm that had perfected a machine to recover "micron-sized gold from the black sands of the western mountains."

The letter had a phone number in the letterhead, which I called. There was opportunity, I was told (if I acted quickly), to increase my shares in this solid gold bonanza. "The machine is running right here in Denver, in a gravel pit, making hundreds of dollars an hour," I was assured.

He didn't seem to want to talk about divers and the sunken gold, and it seems the taxes on the greenhouse were prohibitive, so I asked for some time to think this all over. He hung up.

Well, I've got this friend in Denver, old Clint Eddy. I called him, explaining this opportunity. He must have had the TV set onto some funny show because he almost choked from laughing so hard.

34

I said I wished he would share the humor, which generated something sounding like a guffaw.

"What," he asked, between muffled sobbing sounds, "is the address of this place?"

I said I wasn't sure gravel pits had addresses in Colorado, but the company was located … I read off the address.

He called back a week later.

The gist of his conversation was simple: the address was an empty field.

Recently, another year later, came another letter. If I will send in my certificate, it promised, I'll get back one quarter as many shares in a bottled spring water company in New Jersey.

It turns out this is the growth industry of the 1990s and I'm in on the ground floor! I sent in the certificate, registered, return requested.

I got the letter today … the transfer is on hold, pending my sending in a $7 transfer fee.

Good money after bad?

Originally appeared in Lake Superior Magazine, *October/November 1989*

Silver Mining for Fun ... Profit ... and Excitement

"FIRE IN THE HOLE," Jack Strickland's distant yell came through the trees, echoing off the rocky cliff next to me. An old miner's term, it meant the fuse had been ignited. I crawled even further under the clump of fallen trees selected as a hiding place. What would it sound like?

Three sticks of dynamite had been placed in a hole as deep as I could fashion with my hand in an old pile of vegetation and small rocks – "poor rock" it's called – material discarded in the pursuit of a vein of ore or precious metal. In this case, silver.

"BaaRUMP!" came the blast, but before I heard it I sensed the fragments of rock flying through the treetops close at hand. Small bits of leaves were fluttering to the ground as I crawled out from under the logs. Curiosity as to what the blast revealed was paramount; I started up the hill.

We were evaluating the Prince Mine, located at the southwest entrance to Thunder Bay.

Several early explorers had reported "a great white vein reaching under the lake, at the end of an island on the north shore." It was described as being "greater than 12 feet in width, dividing in places."

Colonel John Prince had learned of the famous vein in 1844. Organizing an expedition in Montreal, he led a small group by canoe to the north shore of Lake Superior in 1846. Arriving in early July, they first mined the vein on Spar Island, where ample evidence of their effort still remains. Some silver was found, but Colonel Prince felt the true bonanza lay in the thick forest of the mainland to the northwest.

While his men labored on the island, he and a companion explored the shore, finding the gleaming vein quickly.

Tracing it to the first bluff of rock, they drove a drift, or horizontal tunnel, into the cliff. Again, some silver was found, but not in the quantities expected. Scaling the bluff, they found the vein again in the second tier of cliffs. Again a tunnel was begun, but atop the cliff more silver was found in the exposed vein. This time a shaft was sunk, following, according to his notes, rich silver showings. Despite their efforts, no values were found that would have made mining profitable.

The vein of silver is very evident as it extends into Lake Superior at the Prince Location southwest of Thunder Bay, Ontario. Lake Superior Magazine photo.

The Prince expedition left this hostile place in the fall of 1846, never to return. Colonel Prince did, however, record the claim, and it still shows on maps as the "Prince Location." The original claims were eventually divided, and the mining rights are now separately owned. An old hotel keeper in Port Arthur wound up with the mainland portion, bequeathing it to a dear woman who nursed him in his final days.

Enter Jack Strickland.

I first met Jack in 1970, a prospector who lived with his wife, Helen, on Pine Bay, just across the Canadian border. Over several years, we explored many of Jack's various claims, each one destined to be the place where "we'll strike it rich." Strickland had achieved an agreement with the owner of the Prince Mine, promising to find a mining company to purchase her claim, leaving them both in the lap of wealth for the rest of their lives. He called me.

"Jim," he said, "I've got a major (meaning a larger mining company) almost on the hook for the Prince. If you'll just send me a letter indicating you are interested, I can use this to force them to option the property to keep you from getting it."

To me, it seemed like a small favor for an old and never-quite-successful friend. Thus, I sent the letter, indicating I wished to visit the property with my boat, along with "Tom Erspamer, noted mining engineer from northern Minnesota."

Tom was, at that time, general superintendent of Eveleth Taconite Company's mine. Laying it on just a little thicker, I advised we would be accompanied by Dr. Wayne Samskar, "whose fame, I am sure, is familiar across Canada." I closed with a brief reference to "our intent to retain Dr. Ray Oja to coordinate our efforts." Known as "the Flying Hammer," Oja is a geologist of great note in the Thunder Bay district, having authored dozens of papers on the area. I mailed the letter and dismissed the subject from my mind.

What I didn't know was that Jack Strickland was in trouble. Several major companies had contacted the claim owner directly, rather than deal with Jack, her self-appointed protector. To cement his tenuous connection, Jack had no choice but to show her my letter, and we then became in her eyes a "major mining company." Thus Jack's frantic call and our subsequent visit to the fabled Prince Location.

While to me *Skipper Sam II* is just my boat, it was quite a "yacht" that morning in 1978 when we arrived in Thunder Bay. Tom, dressed for exploration, Wayne similarly outfitted and Dr. Oja, complete with packsack, rock hammer and vocal Finnish friend (female), joined Jack Strickland and the claim holder, who was suitably impressed.

Clearing customs, we set out for the Prince Location.

Exploration of the site led to the decision to "blow" the poor rock piles, gather random samples and have them assayed. I dug several of the holes, Jack was the "Powder Monkey" and Ray Oja made up the fuses and blasting caps. Implicit in such activity is the unanimous understanding that only one charge would be exploded at a time.

We should have known something was amiss earlier in the day, when it was discovered that Jack was carrying the dynamite, fuses and CAPS in the same pack. Oja and Erspamer almost had heart attacks as the components were gingerly separated. In the world of explosives, this is the supreme transgression. The enthusiasm and banter formerly present died abruptly.

Now, the exploratory blast was over and we enthusiastically climbed, seeking the results. Nearing the top of the hill, I sensed, rather than saw, another rock. It came through the trees and sheared a sapling behind me, just missing my head. I felt the rush of air on my face as I tumbled forward, seeking anything resembling shelter. The unannounced second explosion rattled my eardrums, adding to the terror I already felt.

Unbeknownst to us all, Jack had lit two fuses. The colorful language emanating from several directions clearly announced the end of the adventure. We left him there, protesting loudly, as the rest of us made our way through the woods to the beach and the boat.

The Prince mine could wait another 132 years as far as we were concerned. A quiet and less enthusiastic Strickland finally appeared on the beach. It was a chilly ride back to Thunder Bay.

Originally appeared in Lake Superior Magazine, *September/October 1987*

CHAPTER THREE

Poking Around the Shoreline

And the Water Just Went Away, Mommy

The haunted shores of Lake Superior evoke both fear and excitement. The modern day boater, and his landlocked exploring counterpart, have resources our pioneering forebears could scarcely conceive, such as the benefit of weather forecasts.

In the 1850s, a little girl stood on the shore of the St. Marys River in Michigan, not far from the dangerous rapids that would soon spur construction of the first American lock at Sault Ste. Marie. The area was described originally in the French Jesuits' "Relations" sent back to the mother country by her Jesuit sons.

While history records her name as "Cary Anne," it does not give her a last name in the journals I have reviewed.

She was playing along the beach, scarcely conscious of the incredible volume of water passing her. The game was to throw a stick into the rushing water, and then see just how long they could run along the beach, keeping up with it.

Something was wrong. The stick almost stopped! Cary looked around, seeking contact with the other children who, she realized, stood almost transfixed.

The river had slowed and then ceased to move, the former current causing minor eddies around the increasingly exposed rocks. Within moments, the water began to recede toward the west and the giant lake above the river – Lake Superior.

It was, Cary Anne would later recall, absolutely terrifying.

Word spread immediately, and the rush of adults vying for a

clear view of the rapidly
emptying river soon
overwhelmed the children
who remained on the now
crowded beach.

Soon the bones of
long lost boats were exposed
and the more daring ran
toward them, seeking
whatever plunder had
escaped the demands of
the constant river current.

When, some hours
later, the river returned, it
came with a vengeance.
Chronicles of the day
describe it as being a "wall
of water," which appeared
almost without warning,
drowning several in its rush to reclaim its rightful domain.

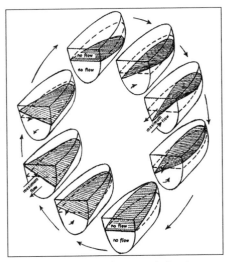

*A seiche behaves much like water sloshing in a pan.
This illustration magnifies the effects on various
shores within a lake. Courtesy Minnesota Sea Grant.*

The phenomenon, more common to Lake Superior than any
other of the Great Lakes, is known as a "seiche" (pronounced
"saysh"). Not to be confused with the tidal activity it mimics, this
term still evokes an occasional smirk from an expert whose length
of credentials exceeds his experience. The generally accepted
explanation blames the presence of a massive low pressure weather
system adjacent to an unusually high barometric pressure weather
system. As these move in tandem over Lake Superior, the water
reacts to the weight of air, or lack of it. Strange things happen!

About 140 years after the Sault Ste. Marie affair, *Skipper Sam II*
was lying at Donn Larson's dock in Cloud Bay, Ontario, the almost
circular hiding place in the evening shadow of Mount Molly, just
north of the Pigeon River on the border with Minnesota.

Donn and his wife, Donna, found this tiny slice of Lake
Superior heaven some years before, and in the ensuing years it has
become their haven of happiness and regeneration.

According to the weather advisories, we should have been
digging a foxhole or two in Donn's yard. The dock is made up of
rock-filled timber cribs, carefully constructed by the legendary Zeb
Renshaw of Cloud Bay in the mid-1970s. Normal depth on the
outside is at least three feet or more, easily accommodating *Skipper
Sam II*, if its stern reaches toward deeper water.

Son Randy noted the change first, drawing my attention to the increasingly exposed wetness of a large rock on the beach near the dock. "At least eight inches are wet," he noted, asking no one in particular, "where in the world is the water going?"

Almost as he spoke, we felt the grounding of *Skipper Sam*'s bow on the gravel bottom. As the water's departure hastened, the boat began to list slightly. It was time to move – and quickly!

But it was too late. *Skipper Sam* was aground! This seiche proved to be just the drop of a foot or so, and it lasted but a few minutes. With the return of the water, the *Sam* again floated easily.

In October 1965, a seiche dropped the water level in Washington Harbor of Isle Royale more than 15 feet, and the water was gone for more than an hour.

A few years ago, Ron Thureen and Louise Leoni were near Sand Island in the Apostles. Their craft is an outboard powered inflatable Zodiac, and their hobbies include both diving and photography. A fast-moving summer storm caught them unprepared as they rounded the west point of Sand Bay.

As lightning flashed across the deadly black storm front, they beached their boat, running for cover. Ron carried the anchor and line with him, burying it in the sand. Torrents of rain followed, finding them settling down in the shelter of the trees.

Turning to Ron in amazement, Louise pointed at the boat,

"The lake is gone," she said. The Zodiac was there, all right, but the water's edge was more than 30 feet behind it. This time the water didn't come back for almost half an hour.

Lest we dismiss this phenomena too quickly, let's speculate that such a seiche was caused by the storm that sank the *Edmund Fitzgerald*. Remember, the captain reported damage after clearing the vicinity of Caribou Island in eastern Lake Superior. The Marine Board of Inquiry dismissed the possibility it might have struck the shoals, which reach out to the north from the island, saying they were too deep.

Do you suppose – just suppose – a seiche might have accompanied that terrible storm on November 10, 1975? Do you suppose this could have grounded the *Fitz* without warning, the next wave freeing it for its date with destiny?

Another peculiarity of our lake. Another unexplained mystery. But the seiche is, indeed, very real.

Originally appeared in Lake Superior Magazine, *February/March 1991*

True Residents of Silver Islet

The long anticipated reopening of the old store at Silver Islet, Ontario, is finally a reality. With supplies again available in this remote village, more summer visitors are taking day trips by driving the winding Sibley Peninsula road to explore this link to history.

Clinging to the rocky shore about 45 miles east of Thunder Bay, the village carefully maintains many of the original miners' log homes. Silver Islet is more than 100 years old, yet the seasonal inhabitants keep vigil over the old silver mine, just a mile offshore. In the 1870s, this tiny rock yielded more than $3.25 million in silver, a bonanza surpassing any silver mine then known.

Ann Drynan, keeper of the Islet House gift shop, shares stories of her life at Silver Islet, as does Bob Faithful, whose home at one time was the hotel. These are but two of more than 70 summer resident families, all of whom treasure their link with Ontario's mining heritage.

Jamie Crooks, a Thunder Bay pharmacist, undertook the rebuilding of the famous "haunted house" of Silver Islet some years ago. Standing hard against a towering cliff, the house was at one time owned and occupied by Julian Cross, son of James Cross, the last mine captain. It had accommodated many famous people over the years, including Arthur Conan Doyle in 1934.

Poor Jamie Crooks and his family! They knew of the "haunted" legends, stories which had been whispered over campfires for generations and focused on Julian Cross.

A mining engineer, Julian Cross was the man who located the famous and now exhausted Steep Rock Iron Mine near Atikokan, Ontario. He also was a well-known psychic, and it was this skill that had attracted Doyle, a student of, as well as a believer in, this science.

After Julian's death in 1971, settlement of his estate commenced, but the house was not offered for sale. Empty and forlorn, it nourished the legend of being inhabited by "spirits." Years elapsed, but it was never filled with happiness and family as were the neighboring homes. The Crooks still wanted the old house, but problems delayed it being placed on the market. It wore its "haunted house" mantle well.

Julian Cross, the psychic, was the subject of a story which had made the rounds in mining circles for many years. It seems he had a vision of an immense ore body, rich in iron, lying under a lake in the wilderness.

The time was the 1930s, and Cross' mining engineering background gave credence to his claim. With his limited resources, he lacked the wherewithal to begin the search. In addition, the world was in the midst of a terrible economic depression, but he knew the day would come when iron ore would again be in demand.

At this point, the story adds a benefactor, who staked Cross with sufficient capital to begin the search. He was on the next train north, according to his longtime secretary and confidant, Helen Moore Strickland.

In 1938, after two years of fruitless searching, he came out on the crest of a rocky cliff. The panorama of a glacier-carved lake lay at his feet, but in his mind he saw, as if with X-ray vision, the giant body of high grade iron beneath the placid water. He went back to Toronto.

Again, the story goes, the benefactor believed him, and more money was made available. A drill was hauled in by sledge and finally erected on the ice of what by now had been named Steep Rock Lake. Down went the steel bit, seeking first the muddy bottom, then bedrock and finally iron ore.

Incredibly rich iron ore.

With the encouraging pressure of an impending war, the lake was finally drained and mining commenced. In the 1930s, people had to work if they wanted to eat and, before long, a community had been carved out of the forest. Many fortunes which would ultimately affect thousands of people were born in the honest, hard and dirty work of this mine. A rail line followed, and the mine settled down to providing a good living for hundreds of families over dozens of years.

Hugh M. Roberts, the famous Duluth, Minnesota, geologist, did the evaluation and later worked at this incredible property. Stories abound of the effort required to wrest iron from this land, while dealing with weather, a constantly changing work force and demands of a country at war.

Back to Jamie Crooks. He eventually was able to purchase the old house and, with his wife, Mabel, made plans to visit the property.

With good friends Dr. Tom and Connie Heringer, they set out for Silver Islet. It was late October and raining. A cold wind was urging dark clouds across the sky. The house was cold and damp.

The remote village of Silver Islet, Ontario, was under construction in the early 1870s. The general store sits in the center at the top of the picture. The Cross "haunted house" is in the foreground on the right.

Exploring the dusty rooms, they found that cobwebs were everywhere, adorning a few tired bits of furniture. The top floor, they found, had an open floor grate. "Must allow warmth from the kitchen to rise," Jamie observed, peering down at the old wood cook stove.

Kindling a fire in the stove, Mabel spread out their picnic lunch. As the coffee began to perk, they heard the noise. Low moans, heavy breathing. Grinding sounds. After a few moments, the noises stopped.

All four were speechless. Shadows cast by wavering kerosene lamp flame danced on the uneven dirty walls. Finally Jamie spoke.

"We might have made a terrible mistake," he said.

Nervously, they began eating the lunch. About 15 minutes later, the noises began again. This time a forlorn and lonely howl joined the unearthly chorus. They all stood transfixed. Jamie stared at the look of horror on Mabel's face.

"What have we done?" she gasped.

The sounds were interrupted by the ringing of a telephone. Exchanging glances, they were mystified. Silver Islet has no telephones, nor electric power.

The other couple couldn't contain themselves any longer. Bursting into laughter, the truth came out. They had secreted a tape player earlier, during the inspection of the upstairs. Anticipating the visit, Tom and Connie had made up the tape, beginning it with a long and silent period. As a physician, Tom's constant telephone calls were just part of life. They had forgotten the interruption as they had made the tape!

Today the Crooks' summer home at Silver Islet is the happy haven it was supposed to be. But at night, do ghosts and spirits still exchange glances by the cliff?

Originally appeared in Lake Superior Magazine, *December/January 1991*

The Keweenaw's Vintage Locomotive

"Railroad engine! Rusting away in the woods of the Keweenaw Peninsula." The old man's watery eyes tried to focus on the map I was holding, but his wavering finger would not follow his thoughts.

I had noticed him making his way along the road in the village of Ahmeek, just north of Calumet, Michigan. His obvious age implied knowledge, and our conversation had begun in a totally different vein: the sunken ships of the Keweenaw.

"Building's all fallen down," he said. "Just the cement walls protect what's left of her – what the damn kids and scrappies haven't took off her."

It was about 1963, and we were on our first scuba expedition to the wilds of the Upper Peninsula of Michigan, the fabled Copper Country. The way we had heard it, the beaches were literally awarsh (I know it's spelled wrong – but it's the way we pronounced it then) with shipwrecks, old 1927 Chrysler cars and other valuables mentioned only in whispers! Lying there undisturbed, far out in the wilds of Michigan.

Knowing that in just a matter of hours we would become wealthy beyond our wildest dreams, my stopping to talk to the old gentleman evoked a chorus of moans from my companions.

"He'll know the right way to the shipwrecks," I counseled, "and this brief visit will actually save us time."

You've experienced it yourself. You see a remote area on your map, far from where you live, and for some reason you assume it is uninhabited! If, you reason, I don't live there, how can anyone else?

Well, to this group of explorers, the fact that the towns of Houghton, Hancock, Calumet, Laurium and Lake Linden had people just like us living in them came as quite a surprise. Chatting with the old man seemed like the thing to do.

His name was Jack Olson, and he knew little about ships, sunken or afloat, but he had been a railroader for a lifetime, and it was about time someone asked him what he knew!

"Hecla!" He pulled his tired frame erect, suddenly clear eyes literally boring into me, a firm grip grasping my hands. "Hecla and Torch Lake we were, the best damned railroad as ever hauled copper to the fires!

"And all that's left is a few cars and the one locomotive ... rotting away back in the woods.

"Coal was my middle name," he said. "The company bought that damned Rosebud coal, an' id come down all over us every time the Hoghead hit the throttle, but that engine would shoulder any load."

In answer to my questioning glance, he sneered: "We allus called the locomotive a HOG, and the engineer was allus a HOGHEAD! Us firemen – we made everything work."

Before long, the story of the plucky little railroad came alive in our conversation. We were puffing along the Keweenaw waterway. I could smell the acrid sulfur of the smoke, and the periodic hiss of steam startled us, even though we knew it was coming. The clanking of the locomotive as it crossed each joint in the rails caused us to grip the stair railings.

The side-to-side sway seemed to topple us, no matter how carefully we braced our stance. The shovelsful of coal, the slamming door of the boiler, all became familiar.

"But it's over now ... it's gone forever." Like a wave recapturing footprints on a sandy beach, age replaced the momentary fervor of reclaimed youth. Jack was again an old man.

"Naw, I ain't been there in years," he said in answer to my question. "But you can find it." Directions followed.

So much for ships. We spent the whole weekend climbing up and down the famous hills of the Keweenaw. We tracked back over endless grades, long devoid of rail, ending each time in what became a rain-soaked cul-de-sac. If the locomotive existed, it had little to fear from this bunch of adventurers.

Time passed. In the early '70s, I resumed my search alone, learning that old Jack had taken up firing the Lord's locomotives, or perhaps those of the nether world. I didn't find a trace of the missing engine. Other cares gained priority, and the Hecla and Torch Lake again slipped into the shadows, again a forgotten railroad.

September 1988. Jan and I are standing in Greenfield Village, Detroit. Henry Ford's dream, the village is a re-creation of what made America great and what America was in those years of stable currency and honest effort.

The village is adjacent to the Ford Museum, part of what Henry Ford named the Edison Institute after his good friend Thomas Edison.

"Train'll be here in about 10 minutes," the gentleman on the depot platform said. "And it's the right way to see the whole village!" Ho-hum, I thought, another tourist train.

I heard the whistle first, then found myself staring down the
still empty narrow-gauge track. No phony toy train would have the
guts to have such a whistle; better see this! Steam rising in stately
puffs, the engine rounded the curve and finally came to a stop just
in front of me.

"Torch Lake" was painted prominently on the tender, and the
tender bore the gilded letters "H.& T.L.R.R."

Wait a minute! I rushed to the engine, accosting the fireman as
he climbed down from the engine.

Where did this outfit come from? Where did they get off using
such a famous railroad name for a tinhorn tourist train?

Tugging at his red bandanna, the fireman looked me straight in
the eye, with just the merest trace of a smile. He waved his long-
necked oil can toward the engine, pride of skilled knowledge
gracing his mature countenance, his demeanor confident.

"Mister," he said, "this IS the Hecla and Torch Lake
locomotive, not a copy or a fake.

"Some people," he went on, "learned she was rotting away back
in the woods of the Keweenaw, and they went and got her. A bunch
of railroads helped rebuild and get her here, and Greenfield Village
paid for a good bit of the restoration. She was built in1873 and is
now the oldest steam locomotive in regular service in the United
States. And we love her and care for her like a newborn baby!"

Tears in my eyes, I grasped his hand. There was so much I
wanted to say I just couldn't say anything. He understood.

We climbed on the train. The trip and the visit were both memorable, almost beyond description.

If you're near Detroit, don't miss this incredible train ride into history, and don't forget that the locomotive itself constitutes a good piece of the history of Copper Country!

Originally appeared in Lake Superior Magazine, *February/March 1989*

Isle Royale Rainy Afternoon

He was a little fellow – cold, wet and extremely tired. His somewhat bedraggled scout kerchief had obviously seen duty wiping sweat and probably an errant nose. His slumping shoulders gamely bore the dripping frame and pack; the bedroll lashed atop the pack reached above his head. He collapsed on the dock in sort of a spiral fashion, emerging from this odd performance with a bounce – sans pack frame.

The rest of his troop stood part way up the hill at Isle Royale's McCargoe Cove campsite, silently watching his diplomatic effort at establishing contact with the boat lying alongside the dock.

The cold rain continued to fall, dripping off his hat unnoticed. With a trace of a smile he mustered up his courage, looking me squarely in the eye.

"Nice boat, mister," he observed. "Is it dry in there?"

I assured him that all boats leak, but we did have a few rainfree areas. "Why not come aboard and look it over?" I suggested, stepping back quickly as he leaped into the cabin.

His tiredness evaporated. He was torn between greeting us and making sure the gang on the hill fully realized his accomplishment.

"I'm Billy," he announced, "and I'm from Fort Wayne, Indiana, and I'm hiking Isle Royale with my scout troop, and we're wet and cold and tired, but we're DOING IT!"

His eyes grew even bigger when I handed him a plate of cookies, which began disappearing like ice cubes on a summer sidewalk.

"Better go get your friends," I advised him, "or your life won't be worth a plugged nickel when they find out what you've been doing to those cookies."

He nodded, leaped back on the dock and ran up the hill.

I dug out our big kettle, filled it and began heating some water. A gift from Bob Lang, one of our regular boating companions, we carry it on *Skipper Sam II* for two reasons: boiling spaghetti for seemingly starved Canadians encountered on the Ontario north shore or for heating gallons of bouillon soup for Michigan's Isle Royale hikers. It's done plenty of both.

In no time the whole group was aboard, greetings being exchanged between the consumption of packages of cookies.

Scoutmaster Jack turned out to be an automotive service manager in real life. In no way, he admitted, did his work prepare him for the rigors of hiking Isle Royale. The whole idea of the adventure had been born in the winter comfort of a troop meeting, and the reality of the undertaking had now firmly set in.

As steaming cups of hot soup were passed around, I asked Jack about the decision to hike the island. "We got this map," he said, burrowing in his pocket. "It shows the trails, the campsites, everything...."

With a chuckle, one of the older scouts spoke up, "Everything, except the ravines." The whole group assented with weary laughs. "... Except the ravines," they chorused.

I dug out another large chart (on a boat a map is a chart) and spread it out. The gold, green and brown hues of the geologic relief map of the island brought gasps of amazement. This obviously was new information to the group, and several kneeled down to study the details so clearly displayed.

"Here is the swamp-before-last," one said. "Here is Do-or-Die Hill," said another. Yet another hit the nail on the head.

"Hiking Isle Royale," he observed, "is a whole lot more up and down than horizontal travel."

Scoutmaster Jack pursed his lips and glanced around at the serious faces regarding the map. "What in the world did Mother Nature have in mind," he wondered aloud, "when she made this obstacle course?"

"Jack," I said, "you can take your choice. The Indians and the geologists both have an explanation. The book, *Geology of Isle Royale*, blames it all on the glaciers, the last of which left here about 10,000 years ago. It was just as tough for some folks who preceded you – by about 9,000 years. Their ghosts are still here, guarding their ancient mines, all around us."

The old formula still works, I thought. *Mix scouts and ghosts, and you suddenly have an attentive audience!*

"We really don't know who they were," I continued, "but the late Dr. Roy Drier of Michigan Technological University spent a lifetime trying to solve the mystery."

It is estimated the "mining" work is that of 10,000 men for a thousand years, according to Drier. Thousands of shallow pits or horizontal adits, following elusive veins or masses of copper, dot the island.

Several of these pits have been excavated over the years. In one, a mass of copper weighing several tons was found. It had been freed

Isle Royale, Michigan, geologic relief map.

from the native rock and raised on log cribbing. Another yielded the skeleton of a prehistoric "giant" beaver.

Host rock was cracked and chipped away with egg-shaped boulders, called hammerstones. An additional mystery surrounds these mining tools. Thousands of them were found on the Keweenaw Peninsula of Upper Michigan, almost all having a groove around them, probably to aid in affixing a handle of some form. The hammerstones of Isle Royale, though used for the same purpose, lack the grooves.

"Ghosts or no ghosts" said little Billy, "I'll hike, but mining copper with a stone – no thanks."

"The Indians have a much more interesting tale," I said.

Jack Strickland, an old prospector who lived on the Canadian north shore of Lake Superior, passed the story on years ago. It seems that Thunder Cape, whose high cliffs and rocky shores form the east side of Thunder Bay, was once home to a giant eagle. Early men came to the cape and the islands nearby to steal gold, silver and copper. This infuriated the eagle, since it felt these treasures belonged to the Ojibway people who lived in the area.

While flying high above Isle Royale one day, the eagle saw many men laboring on the island, tearing bits of copper from the rocky hills. Swooping down, it raked the island with its giant talons, seeking to destroy this force of men who would defile the eagle's territory. They fled in terror, leaving only the pits and broken rock to mark their efforts. The eagle scratched the hills and cliffs until it was sure not a single person remained on the island.

Manitou, a great Indian spirit, was pleased. When the eagle finally died, Manitou reformed Thunder Cape into the shape of an eagle's head as an eternal memorial. It remains so today.

The scouts quickly agreed that the Indian tale made far more sense. We discussed the nearby Minong Copper Mine they would have the chance to explore the next day. Scoutmaster Jack noted that some of the prehistoric mining areas would also be visible during their ascent to the Minong Ridge trail.

"Okay boys," he said, "let's get set up in the shelters."

We parted friends, with a strong bond between us: Isle Royale.

Originally appeared in Lake Superior Magazine, *September/October 1988*

Those Wonderful Canadians

With pent-up enthusiasm, *Skipper Sam II* responded to the swells of the dying northeast blow. Summer vacation had begun; we were off at last for the top of Lake Superior.

The continuously fascinating panorama of Lake Superior's north shore unwound on our port beam. Fenders were stowed, lines inspected one more time, pots of fresh coffee delivered to the bridge. At last, it was summer (1992).

After a few hours of sleep on the Knife River Marina transient dock, courtesy of gracious managers Sandy and Pete Bugge, we were again under way as the sun saluted another lovely day. Two Harbors flashed its light at us; Silver Bay came and went; youngsters waved from high atop Palisade Head. We cruised through Taconite Harbor, waved at Lutsen's guests on their decks and finally found the fuel dock at Grand Marais' tiny marina.

Having given at least lip service to the concept of "Global Warming," we all remarked at the very real need – even in the sun – of at least two shirts or a good warm jacket.

Up early again, we noted that the 34 miles to Voyageurs Marina at Grand Portage, Minnesota, passed quickly. Kathy Melby and her brother, "Kek," have this operation on a roll – new docks, spanking clean facilities and even a tiny gift shop. Taking a vote, our crew opted for Isle Royale rather than a direct route to Thunder Bay, and we were soon under way. Once clear of the towering landscape, the cold again set in and jackets were hurriedly donned.

Settled in the beauty of Chippewa Harbor – the twin lakes hidden on the northeast coast of the island – welcome radio calls confirmed that our friends on BlueJay would soon join us. Mike and Mary Lee Lalich and their son, Michael, had left Duluth that morning, a calm lake encouraging good traveling speeds. Soon we were rafted alongside each other, catching up on news and planning the next leg.

After a stop at Rock Harbor, we made a sentimental journey through Merritt's Lane and around the eastern tip of Isle Royale, setting a course for Thunder Bay. For those of you who follow this periodic discourse, age and ill health finally claimed Glen Merritt, but long after his store of knowledge was passed on to his son,

Grant. Studying their tree-cloistered island, I tipped my hat to Glen's image, so clear in my mind, with his welcoming smile and his fishing fly-covered hat.

Another day of flat water, coupled with bracing cold, followed. We elected the route through Spar Channel, staring again in amazement at the wide vein of calcite, quartz and barite. It was here on the Canadian shore that it all began in 1846. I reminded the crew of how the promise of silver, which was found in small quantities in this vein, followed fur as the lure to attract thousands. Thunder Bay began as a supporting settlement called "the Station" for the mines which once dotted the area.

After fuel and an assault on the fantastic Safeway Supermarket, we embarked for Silver Islet. Thunder Bay is well named, and few crossings are made without significant waves challenging your passage. We had it all – sunshine, big seas and bracing cold wind. Only the majestic Sibley Peninsula, better known as the "Sleeping Giant," lured us on. We rounded her tip and found the security of Silver Islet. Chatting on the radio with Mike, I suggested they might like to examine the tiny islet, all that remains of the old mine.

We secured *Skipper Sam* to the dock and soon were looking up at a very quiet Mike Lalich. He'd seen far too much of the old mine site, as his starboard propeller could testify. It had come out a distant second in an encounter with the island's western reef. A problem, but not a disaster. All three blades were still there, but significantly redesigned.

We pressed on, Mike's other engine easily keeping pace with *Sam's* slower speed. Again the beauty of the Lake Superior Canadian north shore held us in its embrace. While Mike and Mary Lee were disappointed by the damage, they spoke again and again of the constantly changing vista, excitement evident in their voices. Only the best of boaters accept such a setback with a smile, and it was a happy crew who tied up near Paradise Island for the night.

Mike's composure was further challenged the next morning, when the usual cold was framed in zero-visibility fog. Handling a boat with two engines (we call this "twin screws") is one thing, but one engine, unfamiliar water and only a little help from the other damaged prop require concentration.

With the help of radar and radio navigation, we made it to Rossport, barely seeing anything else. Tying to the dock, we were met by a welcoming party that included Judge George Paradise, Ray Kenney, Ned Basher and his son, Bret.

Jim Marshall (left) watches as scuba diver Jim van den Ende (center) and Robert Beauregard (right) team up to repair Mike Lalich's broken propeller, proving once again that foreign aid is not expendable. Lake Superior Magazine photo.

Jim van den Ende, whose wife runs the Treasure Trove gift shop, was accompanied by Robert Beauregard, comprising our next round of visitors. The men described the new homes they were building around the community. Rossport is increasingly viewed as an ideal summer retirement area, and Jim and Robert are building quality homes of all sizes.

Introducing Mike and Mary Lee, I explained the damaged propeller.

"Not a problem," said Jim van den Ende. "I've got full scuba gear. Get another propeller on its way and I'll change them."

Not so easy. A propeller of the proper size, pitch and turning direction wasn't available, even after dozens of telephone calls. But Robert came back to the dock, smiling broadly.

"Hey Jim," he chuckled. "Don't you remember what I did for a living?"

I had known him as a grocer, though his store had long since closed.

"I'm a licensed body repair man," he said, "and I know metal. Let's get that prop off and fix it."

Before long Jim arrived in his scuba gear, tank and all. The job was not without incident, but soon the propeller – or what had been a propeller – was on the dock. Robert Beauregard picked it up, examined it and started for his truck. Examining the circle of expectant faces, he smiled and said, "I'll be back soon."

And he was back – in less than two hours. The propeller, except for the coat of bright green fluorescent paint he claimed would scare off any reef, looked almost new. The circle of faces stared in amazement. Not only was the shape of the three blades uniform, he had brazed a broken blade segment into place.

Jim soon had the propeller back on the boat, at which time several offers of compensation came from various directions. Exchanging glances, Jim nodded as Robert declined any form of payment.

"We know you folks would do the same for us," he said, "and we really appreciate you all coming to Rossport!"

We started out for the Slate Islands, continuing our adventure. The broad smile on Mike's face said it all. He had two engines again!

As I say at the beginning of this story, "Those wonderful Canadians!"

Originally appeared in Lake Superior Magazine, *October/November 1992*

CHAPTER FOUR

Memories of Old Friends

Citizenship Doesn't Always Come Easy!

'How old are you, Sonny?" Raising his eyes from the shoe he was stitching, George Paradise studied the truant officer with a questioning look.

In Greek, his godfather said to him, "You know numbers, say 16."

George responded with the word "sixteen," looking the officer straight in the eye.

"You've got to be in school," the officer said, taking him by the hand. When this turn of events was translated to him, George remembers thinking, *this is why I came here!*

Judge George Paradise was born in Vizare, on the Greek island of Crete, in 1897. Seeking more education than the island offered, he convinced his father to send him to America just after his 16th birthday. After a terrible ocean voyage with long weeks of seasickness, he arrived in his new country. Then it was a train ride to Sioux City, Iowa, where he was to join his godfather in the shoe repair business. The language was mystifying, but the enthusiasm of his adopted country was contagious.

Without ceremony, the inquiring truant officer brought him to the high school, where he and other students soon found communication possible. After but a year, George gained admission to Morningside College in Sioux City, soon amplifying his learning capacity with an increasing command of the English language.

World War I interrupted his studies, but service in the military seemed a small price for the opportunities he had discovered. His military service was a source of pride for George, which he often mentioned in the ensuing years.

From Morningside, he gained admission to the University of Minnesota Law School, graduating with honors in 1927. George Paradise loved his new country, and the hours of work demanded to pursue his education were incidental, as he saw it.

He had fallen in love with Minneapolis, but he returned to Sioux City, where he blended a growing law practice with an increasing role in the American Legion. He went on to become the Commander of the Iowa American Legion in 1940, the same year he met and married Creola Hess.

A highlight of his dedicated Legion service came in the late-1940s when he was in Washington, D.C., for a special meeting. George was asked if he would like to meet President Truman, an invitation he quickly accepted. They arrived at the White House while the president was eating breakfast in the family quarters.

After some small talk, the president said, "You've got a heavenly name, but a hell of a political party."

George still is not sure just how Harry Truman knew he was an Iowa Republican!

It had been a long trip. For many, a lifetime.

A long trip that would eventually lead Judge Paradise to the north shore of Lake Superior for the first time in 1950, stopping first in Duluth, Minnesota, then on to Two Harbors. He and his wife drove to Grand Marais, then on to Port Arthur in Ontario and finally, Nipigon. While a rude cabin was available "with a tin roof," no food was to be had.

"Go to Rossport" was the advice, and down the dusty gravel road they went.

Rossport, Ontario, was love at first sight, a charm it still exercises over the wandering visitor. Renting a small accommodation, the immigrant-turned-attorney, turned-judge, settled down to inspect his new vacation area, which he realized carried his name!

That first-year trip to Lake Superior must have been quite an adventure for a couple from the farm country. Staying at a small cabin owned by Jack Spillette, on what is now the highway through Rossport, George inquired about a guide to take him out on the lake:

"Art Spillette is your man," he was advised. "He is an old game warden and knows these islands and the lake well."

Art Spillette had a couple of other traits George Paradise didn't know about, namely his absolutely unruffled calm in any circumstance and the fact that nothing impressed him. He just didn't get excited.

They went out to St. Ignace Island, to a small harbor known to Art. As night fell, they managed to catch several brook trout in one of the three streams which flow into this harbor. It was time for bed in the small tent Art had brought along.

On awakening, George realized that Art had a fire going, and he crawled from the tent. Glancing around, George saw a large black bear making his way toward them on the beach. Momentarily terrified, he cried out to get his guide's attention.

Judge George Paradise

"A bear, Art! A bear is coming down the beach!"

Looking around, Art studied the bear for a moment, and then resumed cooking the trout. He dug into the breast pocket of his shirt.

"Art," pleaded George, "the bear is almost here."

It seemed that Art only cared for the trout in the pan, finally glancing again toward the huge animal, now but a few yards from the camp. He reached toward the fire, with the large firecracker he had taken from his pocket. As the fuse sparkled, he tossed it toward the bear.

The animal was fascinated, pausing to study the smoking and sputtering fuse. As the firecracker exploded, the bear jumped, turned and ran. "All in one motion," George later described it.

In later conversations, George made one point clear. "Always throw the firecracker between you and the bear, not BEHIND him."

After a long and distinguished career, Judge Paradise took a mandatory retirement in 1972, since he was 75. In his mind, this allowed him more time on the north shore, more time in his favorite summertime haunt.

61

While 1992 marked the 42nd year he has come to our lake, 1991 was especially noted. His good friend Ray Kenney, former Rossport schoolmaster and longtime charter fisherman, insisted that George come to the Annual Fishing Derby meeting.

"No need to," George protested. "That is precisely why I retired, so I won't have to listen to more foolishness from foolish men."

He went to the meeting, anyhow.

After several speeches extolling his many attributes, the room fell silent.

"Come forward, Judge Paradise," said the leader of the meeting. "This is for you!" He held up a plaque.

Reading it over, tears came to George's eyes. "Honorary Citizen of Rossport," the plaque proclaimed.

Holding it up, George turned to the gallery of assembled neighbors. "Are you sure it shouldn't be ORNERY citizen of Rossport?"

Everyone clapped, rising in respect for this fine man, this good friend, this neighbor. It had taken 41 years, he recalled, but "they accepted me!"

Originally appeared in Lake Superior Magazine, *June/July 1992*

The Barnums of Isle Royale

Watching us expectantly, the sea gull finally spreads its wings and takes flight. Its attitude is mirrored in its sharp-eyed glance as it flies past.

"You've got the whole lake for that boat of yours," it seems to be saying. "Why do you have to disturb my fishing spot?"

Checking *Skipper Sam II* down, we drop anchor in this bit of paradise, the bight formed between Barnum's Island and larger Washington Island. In company with Booth and Grace islands, they divide the southwestern end of Isle Royale into Washington and Grace harbors.

As the serenity of the scene invades our minds, conversation is momentarily stilled. Our crew knows the little harbor well. Glances run from the Martin family's little dock to the several Sivertson boats scattered along Washington Island. The Sivertson fish houses look as well kept as last year, and Enar and Betty Strom's boat nestles against their dock on Barnum Island. All is well, we agree, with a tip of the hat to the hallowed memories of Art Sivertson, Einar Ekmark, Rodney Martin and dock builder Marshall Chabot.

From the cluster of docks and boathouses on the southern end of Barnum's Island, a small boat emerges. Standing in the stern, a skilled hand guiding the outboard engine, George Grenville Barnum, his wife, Elizabeth, and his charming guests are soon alongside. With his infectious smile, George performs the annual rite of welcoming us to his island world.

Long before Isle Royale became a National Park in 1940, many families had homesteaded, raised families, mined and fished here. It was around 1890 that George's grandfather became interested in Isle Royale and subsequently acquired an island. He purchased the property from John E. and Will Johns, longtime Isle Royale residents. These two fishermen owned the *Crescent*, a passenger and fish boat that traveled between Isle Royale and Duluth. The welcome funds they received for their "extra" island came in mighty handy.

George Grenville Barnum was a man of wealth and dignity. He had earned his wealth the hard way, often walking the many miles between Duluth and Minneapolis as he helped build the Lake Superior and Mississippi Railroad. Later activities led him into the world of grain trading. He was one of the founders of the Duluth Board of Trade.

As the new century dawned, Lake Superior became the hub of commerce almost undreamed of just a few years earlier. A small settlement grew on Barnum Island, becoming the gathering place for men of commerce who sought the peace and challenge of good fishing that the island provided. A younger Johns – Edgar – provided skilled fishing assistance and also looked after the property as needed. He became master of *Halcyon I*, a double-ended gas-powered boat, the main means of transportation between Grand Portage, Minnesota, and Isle Royale.

Progress was observed on a rocky reef a few miles to the southwest. To a tiny community accustomed to hand labor, construction of Rock of Ages Lighthouse seemed impossible, but it happened quickly. The first lighting of this sentinel of safety in 1909 was cause for quite a celebration.

As the years passed, the elder Barnum's visits decreased, but his son, George Grenville Barnum II, found more reasons to seek the solace of Isle Royale. He commissioned the construction of *Halcyon II*, a 42-foot twin-engined yacht, which was built in Duluth. Edgar Johns was pressed into service, running the new and faster boat between Duluth and the island. George didn't care for long bouts of water travel, so he would meet the boat at Grand Portage for the 18-mile trip to the island.

The families of Isle Royale found the Great Depression of the 1930s particularly galling, since even if their nets were full, the catch was almost worthless. While they could provide food for themselves, there was little credit for clothing, fuel and needed nets. Through those difficult years, a strong bond of friendship held the next generation of youth.

Prohibition made certain types of income available to those who understood the lake and felt comfortable on its expanse. Canada was but a few miles away, and an obvious source for the spirits many Americans were more than willing to pay for. The famous aviator "Dusty" Rhodes, flying his *Spirit of St. Louis County* floatplane, was reputed to have participated in many "flights of the spirits." He often found a stop at Barnums Island at Isle Royale a pleasant respite.

With the creation of Isle Royale National Park in 1940, the United States began buying up the private holdings on the island.

A visit from famed aviator Dusty Rhodes around 1930 drew the interested crowd of (from left) George Barnum II, George Sr. and Carver Richards, with young George III approaching. Barnum Family Collection.

While title usually passed for an amount of cash, in the case of vague titles long-term negotiations were initiated. Many families elected to accept a "life estate" in their property, with little or no cash as part of the settlement.

Full use of the property would remain for anyone in the family who was alive before 1940. The Barnums, Sivertsons, Johns and dozens of other families elected to take the life estate option from the National Park Service, while almost all of the commercial resorts were glad to sell and put the economic devastation of the Depression behind them.

A sad chapter in the history of the island occurred in the first years of the park. Fire was used extensively to remove buildings and equipment. Singer's large hotel, just across from Barnums on Washington Island, and Belle Isle Resort were but two of dozens of properties that fell to the torch of the new caretakers. Hard feelings, bordering on hatred, grew out of those stormy years.

There followed a period of accommodation, where the life estate families became acquainted with the park administration, and the rangers got to know the families. The Park Service realized that the families were interested in preserving the magic quality of Isle Royale and differences diminished. The NPS went to

Barnum Island commands a view of the southwest from Isle Royale. This circa 1910 photo shows many of the Barnum family dwellings, plus Singer Hotel on Washington Island in the foreground, which was later removed by the U.S. Park Service. Barnum Family Collection.

considerable effort to record the histories available from the families, and a museum was created at Park Service headquarters on Mott Island.

Across from Barnum's, the Sivertsons continued to fish commercially until the sea lamprey decimated the trout population of Lake Superior and made fishing unprofitable. Stanley Sivertson resumed after the lamprey was controlled, but the number of fish he could take was controlled by the state of Michigan.

Isle Royale National Park faces the new challenge of what to do with the old properties as, one by one, the life estate agreements run out. The park's superintendent also must cope with a myriad of regulations, ranging from spilled gasoline and oil at boat fueling facilities to a growing demand for more services. Water and sewer capacity is about at its limit at the Rock Harbor facility, and plans are being considered to reduce this pressure.

George Barnum's view from the porch of his cabin is over the fishing grounds surrounding Rock of Ages Light, at the southwest end of Isle Royale. He is familiar with the increasing sportfishing pressure. But he is quick to point out how long-term seasonal residents help keep the quality of the park intact, acting as "stewards" by their very presence.

George feels strongly that some arrangement should be possible whereby families with long-term ties to the island are able to retain use of the family properties. The use would probably be limited, including maintenance of the existing structures only, but the rich lore and treasured memories might be passed on to those interested.

Skipper Sam II makes for the open lake, another visit to Isle Royale history. On Barnum Island, a figure raises a hand in farewell. As we wave back in return, the picture of George Grenville

Barnum III etches in my mind. Like so many we've met at the Island, they just seem to belong there!

Originally appeared in Lake Superior Magazine, *October/November 1993*

Note: George Grenville Barnum passed away in 1998, but his image at the dock on Barnum Island is just too vivid to fade from my mind.

An Old Harbor Master Is Gone

The original *Skipper Sam* was still new to me that day in 1966 as we rounded Bark Point en route to Bayfield, Wisconsin. Everyone from western Lake Superior went to Bayfield in those days (goodness, I'm beginning to sound old), and the intermediate stop was Cornucopia, Wisconsin, about 50 miles from Duluth-Superior.

Bark Point, reaching out into the lake, shields the whole of Bark and Siskiwit bays from northwesterly weather. Nestled in Siskiwit Bay, Cornucopia has been home to commercial fishermen since before the turn of the century. Old pilings mark the early and futile attempts to add a dock to the sandy shoreline.

I just happened to look down as we rounded the point. The sandstone real estate sliding by just below the surface seemed to be but inches below the solid oak keel of our 38-foot Petersen glorified fish or work boat. Bark Point reef, as Emory Jones would later explain, laid in wait for any unsuspecting soul with a watercraft who either didn't have a good chart or didn't read the one available. It is easy to avoid, we now know, by either staying within a few feet of the point as you go around or by clearing it by a quarter mile. Once past the shoal, the welcome shelter of Cornucopia Harbor beckons to the traveler.

Entering Cornucopia involves two parallel piers, the eastern sheet-piled structure angled at its outer end toward the western (shorter) pier to provide a totally sheltered entrance if the wind should happen to be from the northeast. A flashing green light marks the entry.

We idled into the tiny harbor, dusk overtaking the fleeting rays of sunlight. Finding space along the rude dockage, we tied up under the watchful gaze of a small gentleman who obviously was in charge of these surroundings. Once we were secure, the little man asserted himself with the remark that he would fill our gas tank in the morning. Climbing into an old pickup truck, he disappeared.

Thus began a relationship which paralleled dozens of similar educational experiences known to other boaters who had come to know Emory Jones of Cornucopia.

Emory Jones (right) visits Jim Marshall on the Skipper Sam II *while docked in Cornucopia, Wisconsin. Emory ran the harbor with determination.* Lake Superior Magazine *photo.*

Emory would, when in a reflective mood, describe his adventures, which was his way of sharing the teaching experience. He found a certain kindred spirit with power boaters – the mature outgrowth of gas-powered fishing boats – realizing that they accepted real marine progress since the days of indentured seamen and the sailing ship. He would stand with one hand holding the rail of his well-dried-out 26-foot pond net boat, carefully cradled for years alongside his rough "office."

Often, with a sigh, he would describe his puny attempts to penetrate the totally closed and absolutely inflexible mind of sailboater Roeland Reyers. He felt that Reyers had been born clutching a cotton rag, leading to the further compromise of common sense, making a diehard sailor out of him.

"He'll come," Emory was often heard to say, "when the darn keel of that funny boat finds one too many reefs."

Not all power boaters met with Emory's approval. If not a true boater by his standards, the offending transient would be asked to leave, often unaware of just what sin had been committed.

Garbage, beer cans and glass bottles had only one place in Cornucopia and could never be where tiny youngsters might step on them. These same youngsters had better have a life jacket on when near the docks or they would learn very quickly how short Emory's temper could be.

Fritz and Wally Kolquist, Al Youngberg and Mel Maust were but a few who did meet with approval. Don Stanius built a trailer park which attracted a whole team of enthusiasts. Hollis Nicholson moored a boat in Emory's marina for years.

Emory fed legions of ducks each year to the point that entering the tiny harbor at less than dead slow threatened what seemed to be the entire mallard race. We laughed one year when he converted the fish smoking shed into a jail to punish one really ornery mallard drake.

"That ought to teach you," was the outburst as Emory threw the bird into the pine slab edifice, slamming the door almost off its tired hinges.

When a chance remained that the commercial fishermen would again be able to fish, Emory stored their boats at the end of a railway, running his pickup in tight circles around the winch that would haul them to the safety of dry land before the gales of November.

The years passed and our visits began to include offering breakfast and several cups of coffee to an increasingly lonely little man.

Look around you! Just who is it you take for granted in your reasonably well-ordered life? Take a moment, tomorrow, to tell that person just how much you appreciate him or her. And, more important, just how much you appreciate what they have taught you! Perhaps it won't be comfortable, it might even be embarrassing, but do it.

Emory Jones is gone, but I'll guarantee you he is not forgotten. He died in 1989. We speak for many when we say we still miss him.

Originally appeared in Lake Superior Magazine, *June/July 1991*

Herb Melby, the Boater's Friend

'Okay, Skipper Sam. We'll be looking for you to arrive by..."
Herb Melby's voice, always calm, almost laconic, reached across
the 18 storm-tossed miles of water between us. We were leaving Isle
Royale's North Gap, the tiny band of water that separates Thompson
Island from the main island. The darkening skies had appeared
without warning – it would be another less-than-placid crossing
from Isle Royale to Grand Portage Bay on the Minnesota shore.

By the time we made landfall at Hat Point, entering the relative
calm of Portage Bay, eight other boats would find comfort in our
wake. And, with Herb's moral support, another safe crossing.

Had trouble arisen, Herb Melby's 16-foot Bertram high
performance boat would have been at our side. Had the seas been
excessive, he would have suggested that we consider carefully the
logic of staying on Isle Royale one more day.

With knowledge attained from 70 years plus of living on Lake
Superior and skills passed on from generations of north shore
anglers, he was simply the best. He kept track of customers and
friends, nominally including almost anyone boating northeast of
Grand Marais, Minnesota.

Located just southwest of the Canadian border, Grand Portage
Bay fills a unique role on the north shore. It was here that the
Montreal Voyageurs rendezvoused with the traders of the far north.
In the 1960s, before Herb established Voyageurs Marina, we who
sought to explore or dive Isle Royale had no choice but to launch
our trailered boats on the east shore of the bay, near remains of a
100-year-old dock. If the lake were rough, we "waited for weather"
with a short hike to visit the famed Witch Tree of voyageur diary fame.

Herb acquired this land in 1967, finding himself a caretaker of
those trying to visit the island. He repaired the old dock and added
a stronger system, providing safe shelter for the Sivertson Fisheries
mail boat. Captain Roy Oberg lived nearby, enjoying the brief walk
to his vessel, warming the *Voyageur* for its three-times-a-week, two-
day trip to the island.

Herb, having retired from a career with Reserve Mining, built a
home on the property. Then came a small motel, restaurant and

71

expanded secure parking area. The boat launching business prospered, as word spread that Herb really cared for his boating customers. His wife, Faye, kept the books, trying to balance Herb's major expenses for dredging, deeply footed docks and a miscreant sewer system with the brief two-month launching season.

The summer crew was supported by regular visits from daughter Kathy, an interior decorator in New York. Son C.H., known to all as "Kek," also left his responsibilities as a colonel in the U.S. Air Force to pitch in for a few weeks. In later years, Kek's son, Drew, spent summers, and Herb's sister, Elsie Melby of Duluth, was a regular "working" visitor. Elsie is better known now as the Norwegian Consul Emeritus of Minnesota.

Herb's concern for boaters has generated a host of stories, but I'll share just one to illustrate. Some years ago, a prominent Duluthian arrived at the marina and prepared to launch his new boat. Herb looked over the fellow's boat and his guests' clothing, suggesting neither were prepared for an outing on Isle Royale.

"What do you know, old fellow?" said the boater. "This is a most expensive boat!"

As he launched the craft and loaded it with provisions, Herb increased his vocal protest.

"Where is the canvas boat top?" Herb asked. "The one that will keep any water out?"

"Best you mind your business," came the reply, "and I'll mind mine." In a calm sea, the group departed for Isle Royale.

It was just a few days later that the call came over the marine radio, a panicky voice pleading for guidance and the help of the Almighty. A late-August storm held northern Lake Superior in its grip. Herb realized that the stricken boat was the inexperienced crew he had talked to just days before.

At last getting them on his radio, they admitted they were "off the north shore," but unsure of where.

With his valiant Bertram no match for the insane seas, Herb stayed on shore, monitoring the calls for help. An ore freighter responded, rounding the end of Isle Royale to provide temporary shelter for the terrified crew's boat. Together, they started for the shelter of the north shore.

The calming seas in the lee of the freighter were but brief respite. As the big ship moved on to the southwest, the little boat and its occupants were left in the exposed sea, just off the southwest entrance to Grand Portage. They were being blown into the most shallow and dangerous part of the bay.

Herb Melby was the master of the harbor in more ways than one at Grand Portage, Minnesota. Lake Superior Magazine *photo.*

Herb had alerted a member of the Grand Portage Ojibway tribe who was experienced on the water. He set out from the bay to assist them – in a smaller boat. The wind and waves challenged, but his skill propelled him toward the stricken vessel.

Despite crashing waves and exposed rocks, the wooded shore must have looked appealing to the terrified crew. "I'll beach her," the stricken captain cried over the radio, heading for the south point of Grand Portage Bay.

"No, absolutely NO!" was Herb's calm radio reply. "The whole southwest point is foul, and you will be lost."

The rushing wind blocked some of his transmission, but his instructions were clear. "Keep her off the rocks – help is coming."

Without benefit of radio, the young rescuer pressed on, finally coming alongside and jumping aboard the endangered boat. He glanced at the terrified and totally immobilized crew, advancing the throttle as he gauged the few remaining yards between the tiny boat and certain destruction. It responded. Within an hour, all were safe ashore and the boat was on its trailer.

"She's for sale," said the owner, pressing another bundle of bills in the young man's hands. "I'll never boat again!" And, he didn't!

Herb shrugged his shoulders, masking a smile of self-satisfaction. Turning toward his daughter, Kathy, he shared a glance so private that only she understood.

How lucky we boaters are. Herb Melby passed away in August 1991, but Kathy Melby and her brother, Kek, plan to be on hand for the summer at Voyageurs Marina, along with Drew and his wife, Robin. We know they will amply fill Herb's shoes.

You all had the finest teacher, and you stuck by him to learn and absorb. We wish you the very best!

Originally appeared in Lake Superior Magazine, *April/May 1992*

Paul Flynn, Hard Hat Diver

Still fully dressed in his canvas diving suit, lacking only his battered brass helmet, he felt the little barge capsizing beneath his feet. The late November storm had come out of nowhere, Paul realized, and now he was headed for the bottom of Lake Superior loaded with weights and iron shoes, and no way to breathe. Icy water, entering the suit through the open metal collar piece, quickly soaked his long underwear.

Twenty feet below the overturned barge, he landed on the bottom, face down and in a kneeling position, astride the large concrete pipe he had been assembling a few minutes before.

His hands found the flange of the pipe joint, indicating the direction to shore. With a crablike crawl, he started for the beach almost 100 feet away. His lungs burned for just one gulp of air. His vision blurred with bright speckles of light as his consciousness deteriorated. The endless sleep beckoned.

Crawling on, he felt the surge of building waves above him, a trough granting him a moment above the surface. Gasping for breath, the next wave pummeled him under, but now the weight of his diving suit added stability.

Pressing on, he made it to the beach. Wind-driven snowflakes swirled around him as he raised his head to stare at the overturned barge.

He forced a smile. Andy, his faithful diving-tender, buoyed by the life vest he constantly wore, was also emerging from the surf. Staring in mutual disbelief, they grabbed for each other.

"We beat her one more time, Andy," Paul whispered, "but this one sure was close."

It was the 12th year of his work as a diver, and Paul J. Flynn glanced upward as he offered his prayer of thanks. They drove home in his old truck, the suit freezing solid along the way. Later, they would finish the job of installing the French River Fish Hatchery water intake, 12 miles north of Duluth, Minnesota.

Despite the scare, he pursued water work as a career spanning more than 40 years.

Paul's father, Captain Cornelius O. "Con" Flynn, had encouraged

Paul Flynn with Andy, his faithful diving-tender.

Paul to join the Navy, where he trained as a diver. After learning how to put on a deep sea diving suit, he was sent down, still filled with enthusiasm. He had secured his diving harness, carefully checking the knot around his chest. What he had not done, he later realized, was check the air hose connection, and he soon found himself on the bottom without the ability to breathe – a lesson learned.

After being jerked to the surface, he was greeted with derisive laughter from his instructor and fellow students. Paul learned the first lesson well: never go down until you are sure everything is RIGHT!

When the steamer *America* sank at Isle Royale on June 7, 1928, Paul was summoned, and his first task was the recovery of a luckless Irish setter from the after deck; the animal had been chained there for the voyage. A complete inspection of the entire hull followed, revealing the damage that had caused the sinking to be a semicircular tear in the hull under the engine. He advised his father that it was a simple repair, which led to Con's bid and subsequent ownership of the sunken vessel. Title passed to Paul in the 1930s.

I first met Paul in 1965, at his home on Skyline Parkway in Duluth, just west of Lake Avenue. Trim and just under six feet tall, he met me with a firm handshake and offered a chair. His lovely wife, Irene, made me feel quite welcome, plying me with coffee and a still-warm cookie as I sat down. The conversation quickly moved to his work and his ownership of the steamer *America*. Over several visits, many an interesting tale of Lake Superior emerged, in addition to the one described above.

While building the south breakwater at Silver Bay, Minnesota, in 1952, Paul found the wreckage of the wooden steamer *Hesper*. This 250-foot wooden steamer had foundered at what is now Silver Bay on May 3, 1905, and had been long forgotten. The rock of the breakwater now covers most of it, but at the time he found it, the wreckage was intact and undisturbed. A large, round brass nameplate, bearing the name *Hesper*, was removed from the wreck and is somewhere around the west end of Lake Superior, but hasn't been seen for years.

In 1931, Paul had been retained by two local men to find the steamer *Kamloops*, which disappeared at Isle Royale in a 1927 storm. Rumor alleged it was loaded with whisky, a valuable cargo during prohibition. With the retainer, he went to Chicago to check the manifest with the insurance underwriters. The cargo was shown to be a paper-making machine, candy and toothpaste, but no whisky was listed.

Relaying the information to his employers, he was unable to daunt them; they said it was obviously a smuggled cargo.

"Oh yeah?" replied Paul. "You fellows better get another diver. The *Kamloops* was a Canadian ship, and they didn't have any prohibition on alcohol."

Paul passed away in 1966, but his stories live on in my tape library. Like so many who depended on our Lake Superior for their livelihood, he was a great and good man.

Originally appeared in Lake Superior Magazine, *May/June 1987*

The Merritts of Isle Royale

Isle Royale, Lake Superior's largest island, continues to fascinate a large segment of the lake's boating population. So much has happened here, I muse, as we cast *Skipper Sam*'s lines off at Rock Harbor on Isle Royale. The rising August sun finds us as we round the old steamer *America*'s dock, heralding a simply beautiful morning. Lines stowed, the crew is sipping coffee and exchanging thoughts about how the day is an example of why we live around Lake Superior.

Our destination of Thunder Bay on the Canadian shore is an easy day run, encouraging a leisurely pace. Approaching Scoville Point, the chart shows the three routes available that can take us to Blake Point, the northeast end of the island. We can continue out of Rock Harbor, beginning our crossing to Canada at North Government Island, or we can use a channel which is really an extension of the deep cut of Tobin's Harbor. It meets the lake just north of the same island.

A third option I describe as "magical" – Merritt's Lane – one of the most scenic passages on Isle Royale. Less than two miles long, this route is between the rocky spine of the main island on the north and several smaller islands. At one time, four of these belonged to Alfred Merritt, one of the legendary "Seven Iron Men" of Minnesota mining history. Our crew is unanimous in its decision: *Skipper Sam*'s wheel is soon hard over to port (left), as we turn at Scoville Point.

Approaching the rugged main island shore, I point out the reefs, one reaching out from Porter's Island, the other a slightly submerged extension of the mainland. Porter's Island is named for a music store owner from Duluth who had camped there, but never owned the property. Easily negotiating the notch between, we turn to the northeast into Merritt's Lane. The evident channel bottom attracts our attention, barely submerged ledges of bedrock encouraging careful piloting. Most of the channel is less than a hundred feet wide, nowhere more than twice that. At times our brass propellers are but inches from the unforgiving bottom.

We who boat have a neat way of measuring the comfort level of our crew and guests. Making passage on a calm stretch of open lake

The Skipper Sam II *negotiates Merritt's Lane at the northeast end of Isle Royale. Merritt Island lies directly in front of the bow. Dave Poirier photo.*

we find some of them reading, some doing exercises, some taking a nap. When the passage is a bit more challenging, because of weather or surroundings, the bridge where the skipper is practicing his boating skills attracts everyone.

On this beautiful morning, in this incredible setting, I do not have to raise my voice. The whole crew is around the command bridge. Everyone, with an occasional glance over the side of the boat, wants to know all about Merritt's Lane.

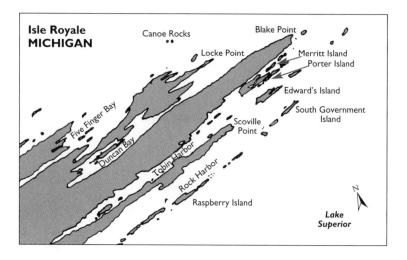

Alfred Merritt passed many years ago, but, until his own death, his son Glen kept his memory alive as if it were yesterday. Appointed Duluth's postmaster in 1933, Glen made a career of assuring that the Merritt name remained unsullied and Glen's son, Grant, continues that vigilance.

A few years before his death, Glen described to me how Alfred first visited Isle Royale in 1866, aboard the schooner *Pierpont*, hauling kegs of salted fish. In 1873, Alfred took a contract to build two miles of road on Isle Royale. It was to connect Siskiwit Bay with the site that would become the Island Mine.

This effort, as Glen described it, "was damn tough going!" The terrain consists of rock and gravel benches of increasing height, forcing Alfred to "hew" this road out of both dense forest and resisting ground. Glen tells of visiting the site years later, and how his father broke into a sweat describing all the effort expended by his crews.

As *Skipper Sam* comes abreast of the larger island, shown on old charts as Merritt's Island, we shut off the engines. Broken only by the occasional call of a distant bird, the almost mystical silence matches that of a midnight campfire in the deep woods. Raising a finger, I point toward the brick fireplace chimney reaching skyward from the dense vegetation of the island. It stands alone, a solemn silent monument to those who built it in 1911. I have carefully considered not even mentioning it in this tale, since misguided forces exist who might take pleasure in its destruction.

The Merritts knew the excitement of discovering iron ore on the Mesabi Range in Minnesota. They knew the risk of building a railroad to Lake Superior over which this ore might move. They knew the nightmare of dissipated finances brought on by the financial panics of those years surrounding 1900.

The Merritts had accepted the proffered "help" of John D. Rockefeller and knew the bitter gall of their notes being called with no resources to meet such commitments. They watched their empire collapse, their homes repossessed, their possessions scattered. They suffered the "I told you so's" of shallow friends who had never risked anything, but had flocked like lemmings to the bar and sideboard of their warm hospitality.

Some say the mistake had been one of ego, insisting that the rail come to Duluth, rather than to the more logical Superior, Wisconsin, harbor. It's of no consequence now, except to the family and those who still admire Americans who thrived on risk.

I explain that Alfred had recouped his fortunes to the degree that he was able to buy these four islands. He paid $10 an acre, $80 for the four, in 1908 at the land sale at Eagle River, Michigan. This was the same sale, incidentally, at which Sam Sivertson and many other "squatters" finally made their homestead claims on Isle Royale valid!

The cabin was built in 1911 and, along with it, an adjacent platform on which a large tent could be pitched. In years to come, when Glen was but a youngster, the ladies slept in the mosquito-free cabin, while the men, with their ever-present cigars, slept in the tent.

In 1940, Isle Royale became a National Park and land acquisition began. This Merritt property was exchanged for a cabin site in Tobin's Harbor, for use by those in the family born before 1940. Fire took the cabin in the 1950s, according to Glen.

Time to engage *Skipper Sam's* engines, as we are drifting almost imperceptibly to the shoreline of the island. Backing away, I suggest that we stand for a moment in silent reverence for this family whose honest effort has earned them a place in American history.

Oh, and please, well-meaning friends of this wilderness, let the chimney stand.

Originally appeared in Lake Superior Magazine, *June/July 1990*

Remembering Isle Royale's Captain Roy

Captain Roy Oberg has retired, ending a long and honorable career with Sivertson Fisheries' Grand Portage and Isle Royale Transportation Company. After more than 2,500 trips from Grand Portage, Minnesota, out to and around Isle Royale, threatening for as long as I can remember that each year was to be his last, 1986 really was Roy's final season and he was honored at a retirement party in Duluth at the end that season in true Isle Royale fashion – a polite way of saying that everyone had an especially good time.

Stanley Sivertson, president of the firm and, perhaps, the only equal Roy might have, said, "Roy Oberg knows the terrain, rocks, islands, currents and reefs around Isle Royale better than any other man, living or dead."

Honest praise for a living legend, all those present were again reminded of the positive influence Roy has had on all with whom he came in contact.

Long before the sophistication of depth finders, radar and Loran, Roy developed courses for traveling in the fog using just his watch and compass. "Travel two minutes, 20 seconds due west, 40 seconds south by west was the way he did it," Sivertson recalled, "and suddenly the dock would be just alongside ... just throw the line on!"

Roy could travel around the whole 55-mile-long island this way, never seeing anything but solid fog. Barrels of salt, nets, milk, newspapers, campers and hikers were his outbound cargoes. Boxes of fish, tired and often seasick Boy Scouts, empty fuel barrels and National Park Service personnel accompanied his return.

Roy's *Voyageur* was all business. Making dozens of stops and quickly pressing on in a most resolute manner, Roy ended Day One of each trip at Rock Harbor on the northeast end of Isle Royale. If you planned to be picked up along the way, it paid to be there at the agreed-upon time. Then Roy would nudge the bow of the boat into the corner where the dock and land joined, and you had better throw your pack and climb on ... quickly! With his good natured chuckle, the boat would already be in reverse, and you tumbled into your seat as the *Voyageur* pressed on.

I first met Roy in 1966 in Grand Portage when a group of us

Captain Roy Oberg knew more about the waters around Isle Royale than any other pilot. Howard Sivertson painting from his book Tales of the Old North Shore.

was engaged in trying to float the 180-foot steamer *America,* which we had acquired "as is and where is" on the bottom of Washington Harbor, Isle Royale. We needed some mattresses, an inexpensive form of caulking to seal the smaller leaks in the hull. Roy had suggested "stop at the store and offer a six-pack for an old mattress, delivered to the dock."

We did this, viewing with awe an ever-growing pile in just a few hours.

"I'd put a rope around them and tow them out," was Roy's advice, "'cause there might just be a few critters homesteading in them that you don't want on your boat." That was excellent advice; the old mattresses almost crawled off the dock by themselves! We couldn't help but wonder, later, just who wound up sleeping on wire springs that winter....

In 1966, with their new recording depth finder, Roy and Merle Otto, engineman and deck hand, located what they were sure was the *Kamloops*, which had disappeared in November 1927. "She is lying in 180 feet of water," Roy said, "just off Twelve O'Clock Point." Sure enough, in 1978 the wreck of the *Kamloops* was located, just north of Todd Harbor, right under Twelve O'Clock Point.

Some years ago I was crossing Siskiwit Bay, on the south side of Isle Royale, in the first *Skipper Sam*, moving through a heavy haze. I was sure we were on a safe course for Chippewa Harbor. We were just able to make out the *Voyageur*, Roy's boat, passing us in the opposite direction and well to our right. Our radio suddenly came to life: "*Skipper Sam*, are you sure you want to hit those reefs just ahead of you?"

There was no mistaking Roy's voice, or the distinctive chuckle which followed. "Turn right, now!" Thoroughly shaken, we did just that, muttering a muffled, "Thanks, Roy," into the microphone.

It was so typical, I later realized. Roy respects the lake and those who use it, and I must be but one of a countless number he has assisted over the years.

On a clearer day the following year, we retraced our course. There they were, two giant reefs that rise from the floor of the bay to within three feet of the surface with no warning. They are named Domen and Doden on the chart and, but for Roy, they might now contain a tiny wreck symbol!

So many Isle Royale families, the Rudes, Holtes, Johnsons, Edisens, Eckmarks, Barnums, Johns and so many others, depended on Roy for their very existence. And, as they will tell you, he was always there.

Roy Oberg is a very special man, a careful blend of skill, knowledge and usually good humor. Somehow, Isle Royale will not feel quite as safe without Roy on the other end of a radio call.

All the best, Captain Oberg!

Originally appeared in Lake Superior Magazine, *January/February 1987*

Note: Captain Roy lived another 10 years after his 1986 retirement.

A Look Back, a Time to Reflect

The steamer *America* hugged the tip of Hat Point at Grand Portage, Minnesota, seeking the shelter of Wauswaugoning Bay on the east side of this promontory. Holding the deck railing with both hands, young Stanley Sivertson shivered in the cold wind as the vessel moved into the bay. On that 1922 Thanksgiving Eve, he wondered why they didn't just strike for his home on Isle Royale, a mere 18 miles away, where dinner and a day off awaited.

If fishing was your business, as it was for the few families who spent most of the year on Isle Royale, a day off was of great significance. Stanley's older brother, Arthur, had learned how nets, lines and weather ruled one's very existence, but on this day on the *America* it was Stan's turn.

His trip to Duluth to accompany their fish shipment and gather winter supplies seemed of great value, and he had felt important. But now, with the Minnesota north shore ports behind him, being home with a day off for Thanksgiving seemed his only reason for living.

Reality asserted itself. Here he was on the pitching deck of the 180-foot steamer *America*. Commanded by Edward C. Smith, one of Lake Superior's best skippers, they were hurriedly seeking shelter from bad weather. It was time to hide on the north shore, time to get an anchor down in a secure and sheltered bay, time to "wait out the storm."

His mind recalled the giant goose which – for some reason – seemed to fly straight across his father Sam's shotgun sight. The quickly defeathered bird took its place under ice and trout filets in the fishhouse at their home on Isle Royale.

On the island, most poultry made it to a plate only after its egg-producing days were over. The largess of a stuffed goose for Thanksgiving was almost beyond measure. The smell of baking bread – the key ingredient of stuffing – graced the house for days. The anticipation of the feast matched every imagination.

As the weather deteriorated, Stan made his way to the pilothouse of the *America*. Rain, mixed with snow, pelted his face as he climbed the ladder. Once inside, he found the first mate and the wheelsman.

Stanley Sivertson, Isle Royale fisherman, spent a lifetime protecting the rights of Isle Royale residents. Mitch Kezar photo.

"We aren't going to the Island?" he asked. Many dots of rock, soil and trees grace the shore of Lake Superior, but the word "island" simply meant Isle Royale to those calling the lake home.

Mate Gust Ege, soon to become captain of this fine vessel, took a deep breath. "Young man," he offered, "you live on Isle Royale and ought to know at least a little bit about the barometer!" Stan's obvious ignorance gained Gust Ege's favor and he reached out for Stanley's hand.

"Look at this, son," he said, pointing to the glass on the pilothouse wall. "Look closely at this number – 29.42 – this is bad weather, and it will get worse!"

Stan nodded, accepting such a low reading as trouble. But, on reflecting on his circumstances, this new information only confirmed that his life so far had been a whole chain of "low readings." Leaving the pilothouse, he made his way aft to the more sheltered deck.

The site we describe is visible as you travel between Duluth, Minnesota, and Thunder Bay, Ontario. Look out at the lake as you start down the last hill from Mount Josephine on Highway 61 while traveling north to Canadian Customs on the Pigeon River. Southbound, you want to find the observation turnout halfway up the first hill south of the border.

The bay, you will find, is deceptive. At first glance, the bay is a wide expanse, bordered on the west side by the high escarpment of Hat Point across from tiny Francis Island on the southeast outer corner. Beyond, to the northeast, the Susie Islands and, on a clear day, Isle Royale is clearly visible in the distance.

Look closely now at what can best be described as the middle of the bay. Watch for a moment and turbulence will be seen, generated as the currents sweeping the bay meet the obstruction of a large reef roughly in the center of the bay. While easy to see from your high vantage point, this reef has claimed a number of vessels over the years as weather and darkness conspired to conceal its presence. On this day before Thanksgiving in 1922, the *America* crew set her anchor well to the northeast of the reef, in good water. The strengthening southwest blow whipped around Hat Point, keeping her tethered to a taut anchor chain, well away from the reef.

Aboard the boat, Chief Engineer Frank MacMillan came out on the afterdeck, gripping the railing with one hand as he sucked on his pipe. Noting the less than secure young Stanley Sivertson, he waved the pipe in a sign of greeting. Stanley was momentarily transfixed, his gaze locked on the remains of Chief MacMillan's right hand. Seeing his interest, the chief thrust it forward.

"Lost it chasing crossheads on an old triple-expansion steam engine," he said, raising his voice to compete with the increasing wind. "Used to have to oil them by hand, and I came out second!"

Stanley was silent. To a young lad, officers of any ship were distant people of great importance, seldom even acknowledging youngsters. Here was the famous chief engineer of the *America* actually talking to him! Gathering his courage, he looked at MacMillan and blurted, "But you play the violin. How?"

The smile on MacMillan's face almost smothered Stanley. "You go in by the piano," he directed, "and I'll go get my violin – and get a good seat, hear?"

As he opened the door to the dining room, Stanley had his second surprise. Another man he had known only as a distant

The steamer America *was the primary mover of people and goods prior to the building of roads along Lake Superior's north shore. This 1918 photo shows the vessel beneath Duluth's Aerial Ferry Bridge. James R. Marshall Collection.*

familiarity sat near the piano, Captain Edward C. Smith. While no smile graced his rugged countenance, the customary scowl was absent and Stanley felt almost welcome.

A plate of thin-sliced and deep fried potatoes sat near the Captain, the traditional recognition by Mrs. Lind of the Captain's presence. "Try one of these," Capt. Smith said with a gesture, encouraging Stan to sit next to him. As Stan took a chip, the boat suddenly heeled and the plate slid slightly. No one else seemed to notice, but to Stan it seemed a very bad omen.

With a flourish, Chief MacMillan appeared, violin and bow in hand. He spoke with the lady at the piano, who began to play. Soon, MacMillan was embellishing her efforts with pure strains, the likes of which Stanley had never heard. In fact, he realized, he had never heard music like this before. With this simple initiation, Stanley Sivertson gained a love for music that would enhance his whole life!

While this small group enjoyed the music, the weather outside deteriorated. What had been a barely perceptible tug as the *America* shifted her strain on the anchor chain had risen to an assertively strong jerk. Capt. Smith hurriedly finished his chips, glancing at the relaxed crew as he rose.

"We might well need steam, Mr. MacMillan," he said, "We might well need steam!"

Music was quickly forgotten and the room emptied, with half-filled plates remaining on the table.

A long walk down the hall and climbing stairs told Stan the motion of the vessel was far more obvious. Once in the pilothouse, Capt. Smith peered into the darkness. Going out on the deck, he found that the southwest wind was history. Gusts were now easily more than 40 miles per hour – and their direction was **east by northeast!** The dreaded reef of Wauswaugoning Bay, he realized, lay scant yards ahead in their path.

Almost transfixed by the potential loss of his vessel, Smith called into the communication tube that connected his bridge to the engine room. "Let go the anchor, chain and all!" Again and again he yelled, hoping against hope that someone had heard him.

They had, and a third assistant engineer made his way forward to the anchor winches in the far bow, two decks down. With a sledge hammer, he smashed the keeper, freeing the chain, which noisily hammered the hawsepipe as it quickly left the ship.

The realization that his command had been heard and his ship was free brought quick action by Capt. Smith. Calling for full power, he stood watch as the *America* gained a degree of distance between her position and the reef seeking to destroy her.

"Take her around Hat Point, Mr. Ege," he directed. "We'll lay at Pete's Island dock in Grand Portage Bay!"

Old Pete's Island forms the main barrier to Grand Portage Harbor, and the remains of his large dock still reach from the beginning of the gravel bar toward the dock at Voyageurs Marina. The *America* rode out this blow secured to Pete's dock, finally delivering Stanley to "the Island" in time to fight over the remains of the dressing and a slice of pumpkin pie.

As quite an assembly of friends bid a final good-bye to Stanley Sivertson some years ago, the services left us in both tears and just a trace of a smile. After a lifetime of defending his fisherman's way of life in a court of civil servants, most of whom could barely even comprehend his great and overwhelming respect for all things natural, Stanley left, unbowed. We who knew this man are better because we did, and his wife, Clara, and his family carry on the proud tradition.

Originally appeared in Lake Superior Magazine, *February/March 1996*

CHAPTER FIVE

The Bounding Main

Summering on the Lake

Some time ago, word got out via an obscure novel that cruising Lake Superior was akin to buying an option on a low-priced funeral. Low-priced, it seemed, because they wouldn't find your bodies. To those of us who spend a good portion of the ice-free months exploring this incredible body of water, this kind of publicity was simply an expression of ignorance. Unfortunately, many readers found it akin to the gospel and changed their boating or other summer plans.

Don't get me wrong. Lake Superior can indeed be violent and overpowering, but in most cases, it will warn you. Any lake that can lay claim to more than 400 wrecks of consequence, and innumerable smaller losses, deserves respect and that's RESPECT in capital letters. The last thing Jim Marshall needs is criticism for having sent novices out on the open lake.

So let's get into some advice. Any sailboater, especially Dave Steffans, an accomplished mariner from the Twin Cities, will quickly claim that wind on Lake Superior is non-existent after Memorial Day. This might be classed as an exaggeration, except that all my sailing friends claim David is the soul of propriety, and his veracity is far beyond reproach.

We real boaters, who with the turn of a key create power and handling characteristics only dreamed of by those who keep North Sails and other vendors of canvas in luxury, accept occasional maritime turbulence.

The remote islands of Lake Superior's north shore are completely accessible to the adventurous boater. Here the Skipper Sam II *anchors inside a tiny inlet for an afternoon siesta.* Lake Superior Magazine *photo.*

In this age of enlightenment, a simple telephone call can get you a weather briefing, and any marina or dock area you select will have this number. Reflect for a moment on your intended voyage. Understand that wind over water means waves; wind over open stretches of water means BIG WAVES. Study, listen and learn. If the larger craft near you postpones its intended voyage, take that decision – really a warning – seriously!

One mutually agreed upon bit of advice: move early, secure your craft before the weather develops and spend the best part of the day in sheltered water or hiking inland.

If your craft is small or new to you, plan in advance to avoid the open expanses of the lake and spend this first summer in relative safety.

The Keweenaw Waterway, accessible from dozens of points of entry, is ideal for your first Lake Superior adventure. Personally, I'd start at Hancock, Michigan's Ripley Marina, immediately east of the Houghton-Hancock bridge, just so I could say I'd met Brach Schnabel. He runs this marina so well that he should start a school for those who think they already know how.

With a 12-foot boat, you now have access to 25 miles of water and more history than you can absorb if you come back for the next 10 years. Listen to Brach, he knows this country and, if time permits, let him suggest a tour of the copper mining historic sites just minutes away. If you are friendly, he will respond. Explore the fishing villages and old docks of the waterway and take enough time to share the legacy of hard work this area reflects with your children or guests.

If the north shore of Lake Superior attracts, launch at Voyageurs Marina at Grand Portage in the shadow of Mount Josephine. Kathy and Kek Melby will be your gracious hosts and their knowledge of the lake will be yours simply by asking. The adjacent Susie Islands are easily accessible, if you learn the trick of moving over the open stretches of water early in the day. Once protected by their little coves and harbors, your small boat, again, is more than adequate.

Many of the boaters we meet each summer are enjoying Isle Royale, having brought their cartops, inflatable boats or kayaks over on the two Sivertson Fisheries daily boats. A call to Sivertsons' Isle Royale Transportation will easily arrange a berth for you, your party and your boat.

If leaving from Copper Harbor or Houghton is more convenient, contact the *Isle Royale Queen* at its Copper Harbor base on the tip of the Keweenaw, or the United States Park Service's *Ranger III* to depart from Houghton.

If adventure is your beat, drive on up to Thunder Bay, Ontario, and launch on any of the several points of access. Now the plot thickens. There is much to explore within the harbor and the "Kam" (Kaministiquia River), such as Old Fort William – a delightful way to spend a day mesmerized by its skillful re-creation of the early 1800s. Visit the adjacent Welcome Islands at your leisure, but only after determining that the expanse of Thunder Bay will lie becalmed for the duration of your voyage.

Since "Thunder Bay" is perhaps the most aptly named sector of the whole lake, take supplies! Though called a "bay," its waters are big and dangerous if stimulated by thunderstorms or a wind of consequence. On those days, park your boat and play tourist in town.

If time permits, explore Amethyst Harbour in the far northeastern corner of Thunder Bay, hard by Caribou Island. The locals call this harbor Keshkaboun. The lovely homes you will see in this area are the result of hard work and great risk by those Canadians who made this wonderful country great.

The tip of the Sibley Peninsula, known in these parts as the Sleeping Giant, is a delightful drive, as long as time is not of the essence. Sleeping Giant Provincial Park can accommodate you and your companions, and Silver Islet, the fabled village of the 1860s, is at the tip of the peninsula. Again, launch your craft and explore, being mindful that you are a guest in some very special water.

If weather seems threatening, act accordingly. This is a fine spot in good weather, but in a disturbance the Silver Islet government dock looks across 200 miles of open water to the southwest. Need I say more?

Nipigon is another mecca for the owner of a modest water craft. Fine docks and sheltered water beckons, along with some of the nicest folks in Canada. Again, smile and say, "Hi." You'll be pleased at the response.

Rossport, Marathon and points east will lure you if time permits. If you make the swing south toward Wawa, don't neglect to put in at Buck's Marina. Fine folks, and the Michipicoten River offers even more challenge, in a safe way.

Most other options in the southeastern corner of the lake require a little more saavy, since Lake Superior flows full and wide to the north. But with a little experience, you'll be able to manage even the winds of Whitefish Point before too long.

For now, load up your favorite craft and accept my challenge – this summer, LAKE SUPERIOR!

Originally appeared in Lake Superior Magazine, *June/July 1993*

Captain Durfee and the Log Boom

Somehow the captains of industry are still remembered. In even a more hallowed way, Great Lakes ore boat captains still command respect.

Oddly, tug captains are largely forgotten, yet they are the real chance takers and life risking is a simple fact of life. Once a line from a large ship is secured to the tow bitt, the large vertical post on the stern of the tug, the strain is taken up. Until their charge is safely secured to the dock, or under way on its own, the tug and its crew is responsible. Working in the shadow of a taunt line, whose parting can cut all of them in half, is just part of a day's work.

Snap they can, and snap they did, as an examination of early newspapers will confirm. It was in this dangerous and challenging environment that Jim Durfee grew up, finally gaining his papers denoting him as a captain of tugs. As he walked to the carline, he wrapped his arms around his chest, the better to contain these invaluable documents. He was known for his ability to position a vessel as needed, and he took pride in doing an exceptional job with whatever vessel he was entrusted.

The Duluth, Minnesota, harbor was a maze of docks, slips and moorings in those days, constantly busy. Steamboats arrived at the Duluth entry in a never-ending stream, each usually towing at least one consort barge, and often as many as three. The barges more often than not were older sailing ship hulls, though dozens of them were built as vessels without power. With a sparse crew for handling lines and cargo, these hulls were destined for a lifetime at the end of a towline. Once in the harbor, the barges were intercepted by the scurrying tug fleet and moved to moorings and docks.

Captain James Durfee was skilled at this work. He was highly regarded for his quick and dependable performance. While the hours were long and a six-day work week was standard, he took great pride in doing what he knew was an exceptional job.

He hadn't earned his nickname yet, in those early years, but crew members talk. Jim Durfee, it became known, had but one problem – fog. In later years he would joke about being called "Foggy," but everyone came to understand this was one weather

James "Foggy" Durfee, like so many tugboat captains, was usually overlooked when it came to accolades. But he earned his nickname rather well. Durfee Family Collection.

condition that he just hated. Mates came to know that fog meant an extra turn for them in the pilothouse. Captain Durfee would find a reason to retire to his cabin, or to be on deck, listening.

One of the more lucrative towing jobs on Lake Superior was moving a boom full of logs from the north to the south shore. These booms were actually a floating enclosure, made up of giant logs three feet in diameter linked together with heavy chain. As the harvesting of northern Minnesota progressed, booms were assembled at Two Harbors, Encampment, Sugarloaf, Cascade and Grand Marais. The latter port proved most durable, the last booms leaving there in the early 1970s.

Tug owners and their captains earnestly solicited a chance to tow the booms, as the growing paper industry had one unique ability: they could pay for the work done! In the first 30 years of this century, economic hardship was a fact of life and cash was king. While speculators held their temporary sway over Wall Street, men labored in the mines for a few dollars a day, and tugs searched far and wide for another day's work.

With wide smiles the order was received to pick up a tow at Grand Marais, and lines were taken aboard as soon as coaling of the tug *Whitney* was finished. Only Jim Durfee was quiet as they cleared the Duluth piers, glancing back at the gathering dark clouds to the northwest. Passage to Grand Marais was without incident, and morning found them but a few miles from their destination. Seeing their smoke on the horizon, the boom crews began the laborious job of closing and filling the boom.

We don't know just how large this particular boom was, but it could well have been more than a quarter mile in length. Using pilings set in place in the harbor and heavy anchor points along the shoreline, the boom was assembled in a rough circle. Pulpwood logs, usually eight feet or 100 inches in length, were dumped into the boom from the wood yard on the east side of the harbor. Load after load splashed into the cold water, gradually filling out the rough circle.

Just outside the harbor, Durfee's *Whitney* lay tied alongside the east breakwater. The late afternoon breeze carried the first wisps of fog, quietly obliterating segments of the shoreline to the southwest. Knowing that they would be under way all night, most of the crew had turned in for some needed rest.

Finally, the foreman came out in his small work tug. Gaining the crew's attention with a brief blast of his high pitched whistle, he told them to back into the harbor. He'd bring them the towline, and they could get under way for Ashland, Wisconsin.

Calling for steam, Durfee gave orders to bring mooring lines aboard. As the *Whitney* began to move, he scanned the scene before him. While the harbor entrance was in full view just ahead of him, little else was visible. He was surrounded, he realized, with thick fog. At the entrance, he called for reverse, backing the tug toward the boom and the towline visible on the little boom tug. Soon it was secured to the big tug's tow bitt, and they began taking a strain on the ungainly mass.

Ashore, the fog embraced men as they untied the boom tethers from pilings and beach anchors. Shouts, muffled by the blinding moisture, confirmed that their work was done. The cold beer of the tavern beckoned. Beach rock rattled in response to heavy boots; pickaroons and other tools of their trade were noisily discarded. The mournful long blast of Durfee's whistle seemed to come from all directions.

Aboard the *Whitney*, visibility was nil. Calling out a heading that would take them across the lake toward the Apostle Islands, Durfee told the mate to "take her," noting their departure time in the log. As the engine labored, activity aboard the tug settled down

Large booms of logs were towed across Lake Superior from one shore to another. Sugarloaf Cove on Lake Superior's Minnesota north shore was a major staging point. Robert Hagman Collection.

for the long voyage. Durfee ate dinner and retired to his small cabin. He had full confidence in his mate, almost offsetting his discomfort spawned by the all pervasive fog. It was time to try to sleep.

No good. Wide awake, he listened to the pounding of the engine, the vibration somehow unfamiliar. Was he really that "spooked" by this unusually thick fog? Maybe a walk around the deck would calm things down. Dressing, he went back up to the pilothouse.

The red gleam of the compass light showed they were on the desired course, the flat lake offering no challenge to maintaining the course. Stepping outside on the deck, he realized visibility was literally zero! The glow of the running lights illuminated the upper rigging, but he had to feel his way aft with the toe of his shoe.

Grasping the heavy towline, he could feel the resistance of the giant boom behind them. All was well, he concluded, and he went back to bed. Sleep was slow in coming.

A large hand was at his shoulder, shaking him gently. "Captain Durfee," said the voice, which he realized was that of his mate. "It's getting daylight, Captain, I thought you might want to get up."

Roused, Durfee dressed, dashing water on his face. Climbing to the pilothouse, he noted a southwest wind had come up and the visibility was improving. Looking about, a shadow to his left startled him. A ship?

The fog continued to dissipate, the shadow gradually became a strange looking tower. How could this be? the crew asked. What is that?

The breeze suddenly cleared the remainder of the fog – the whole crew stared at their surroundings in disbelief.

They were still at the entrance to Grand Marais harbor!

While the land crew had set out to free the boom, they hadn't finished the job because of the fog. Each must have assumed a fellow worker had untied the *Whitney* from the breakwater. Foggy Durfee had pressed on all night, going absolutely nowhere.

Of such stories are nicknames made!

Originally appeared in Lake Superior Magazine, *February/March 1992*

Pleasure Boating?

The next two pieces are offered as cautionary notes, not to scare boaters off Lake Superior, but to remind them that weather on this big lake requires constant vigilance. We can enjoy its many wonders, but we need to keep our ear tuned to marine weather reports and keep our eyes peeled for unusual conditions.

"I don't know how better to tell you this, *Skipper Sam*. We just took a wave over the pilothouse."

The almost disembodied voice, from our marine radio, was followed by an exchange of nervous glances.

Peering into the night darkness, I realized the friendly lights of the freighter *Peter Robertson* were no longer in view. It was apparent that we had gained another passenger on this 42-mile leg from Ontonagon, Michigan, to the upper entry of the Keweenaw Waterway. Apprehension was now on board.

It was 1:20 a.m., July 6, 1976. *Skipper Sam II* was a new boat to our family, a 50-foot cruising houseboat which many dock-bound experts proclaimed "unfit for Lake Superior." This was our first extended cruise, with daughter Cindy, Wayne and Dorothy Samskar and their son, Mark, as crew. We left Duluth, Minnesota, after greeting the Norwegian sailing ship *Christian Radich* on her bicentennial visit.

We completed our fueling at Ontonagon by 9 p.m. The northeast wind had become more evident, but full tanks fueled our optimism as well as our engines. We agreed that the relatively short four-hour run would be more easily negotiated immediately, before the waves really responded to the wind.

With its distinctive bell saying "cling-cling-cling," the Ontonagon River bridge slowly closed behind us. Though still between the breakwater piers, *Skipper Sam II*'s bow lifted, her buoyancy responding to the increasing seas. Passing the pierhead light, we headed for the upper entry. The northeast seas, bending as they do around the giant Keweenaw Peninsula, sported an occasional whitecap.

By 12:30 a.m., we were six miles southwest of the targeted entry, its bright lights offering safety and calm water. A scant half-mile from the sandy shore, our depth finder indicated 40 feet over

Wayne Samskar prepares to kiss the ground following the Skipper Sam II's *harrowing experience on Lake Superior in 1976. His wife, Dorothy, stands behind him. James Marshall Collection.*

the bottom. Suddenly the bright lights of an ore freighter emerged from the waterway, and I reached for my microphone, seeking a friendly voice in the wave-tossed darkness.

The response was immediate. "Hello, *Skipper Sam*. We are the *Peter Robertson*, with owners aboard. We just took the scenic tour of the waterway, as they like to do. We have you in sight and on our radar, five miles southwest." We made a bit of small talk and I signed off, occasionally glancing at their receding lights in the darkness. The entry was just a mile away.

What neither of us knew, in this small moment, was what had happened earlier that night in Duluth. A sudden, intense cyclonic storm had hit the city, severely damaging a number of sailboats racing just offshore. Many of these boats carried members of the cadet crew of the *Christian Radich*. Moving out over the lake, the storm generated, we later learned, a series of giant waves.

Came then the call described at the beginning of this tale.

Thanking the *Robertson* for warning us, we turned and headed out into the lake, desperately trying to get more water under *Skipper Sam's* keel. Waves of such magnitude begin to crest and break as they approach the shore, destroying everything in their path.

Our dozing crew was suddenly wide awake. All doors were secured, life jackets donned and buckled, windows closed and locked. Suddenly we began to rise, as if on an elevator.

Reaching the crest of what we now know was at least a 25-foot wave, the lights of the *Robertson* were again visible, perhaps five miles away. The radio came to life: "We just had a second one; do you need assistance?"

We started down the back of the wave, quickly retarding the throttles and trying to angle our way toward the trough we knew would be ahead.

Wayne was frantically searching for a bottle in which to put his hastily written will. Dorothy was braced in the forward bunk with her hands on the overhead. Mark manned the spotlight control, calm in the face of danger equalling anything previously experienced in his young life.

Reaching the trough amidst a sheet of spray, the boat almost stopped, causing the refrigerator door to fly open and disgorge its contents – including bleu cheese dressing – across the galley floor.

As the wave passed, *Skipper Sam* recovered, facing again the now familiar waves of the northeast sea. I told the *Robertson* we were okay and much appreciated the concern.

Following a quick conference, Mark held the searchlight handle, quickly spotting the second giant wave. We rose with it, topped the crest and began what we now call the "roller coaster ride to hell."

At the bottom of the trough we quickly turned, gaining a position on the back of the wave and powering ourselves to the northeast for better entry position. Only when I could not see the lights of the entry did I grasp just how big these waves were.

I added power, asking Mark to light our way up the foam-flecked wave to the top. Suddenly the lights were visible, almost in front of us. We cascaded between the outer breakwaters, looking down on these normally 12-foot-high piers. We were safe!

In the warm morning sunlight, *Skipper Sam II* seemed to wear a rather haughty countenance and quip, "I told you I could do it." We kissed the ground.

Each season we still get the dockbound queries, "Is she any good in heavy seas?" And each season we answer: "You bet, much better than we are!"

Originally appeared in Lake Superior Magazine, *January/February 1988*

Whither the Weather

With a paroxysm of hesitant barks, the two big Chrysler engines came to life, settling down to a smooth purr as life-giving oil coursed through their steel veins. *Skipper Sam II* gained life at the same moment, nudging gently at the lines that held her to the remains of an old dock we'd found in the north part of Lake Superior.

Our weatherwise first mate Jan appeared on the upper bridge almost immediately, donning her line-handling gloves and acknowledging her understanding in a brief glance. We were in trouble.

Foul weather on the open lake had driven us to the shelter of these tiny islands. Once in the shelter of the cove, a blast of furnacelike heat drove us to shed our extra clothes as we discussed the unusual weather.

Odd clouds, lenslike in shape with a peculiar translucent shading, hurried by. I studied the small thermometer as I wiped my forehead. The air temperature in this remote corner of the lake couldn't be the 94 degrees the instrument claimed, or so I thought.

As if pulling an opaque shade, the sky darkened, obscuring the sun. The increasing wind bore even more intense heat.

The weather forecast out of Thunder Bay, Ontario, had warned us, but with a clear sky and little wind we thought the storm would pass far to the south. Part of our crew still lounged on the deck, only now gathering sunbathing towels with but a glance at the blackening sky. It seemed that the clouds had appeared from nowhere, racing to the northeast, flicking fingers of admonishment at us in our exposed mooring.

To travel safely by pleasure boat on Lake Superior requires but three simple obligations: watch the weather, listen to the weather and FEEL the weather. I'd blown it on all three.

As the engines warmed, the anchoring process was reviewed. Paul, our well-seasoned boatswain (as well as son-in-law), had already made our ground tackle ready.

The first gusts of wind were upon us when the inevitable question was voiced: Why leave a dock when bad weather

The Skipper Sam II *at the Point Porphyry Lighthouse dock on Porphyry Island in Black Bay near Ontario's Sibley Peninsula.* Lake Superior Magazine *photo.*

threatens? Such a question from a first-time guest is almost automatic, stemming from fear as well as curiosity.

Scanning the group, I said, "Look at our dock. The single log we've been tied to can't hold this boat in a blow, and the result might well be our winding up on the beach with our propellers in the rocks!"

Glancing first at the threatening sky and then at the remains of the once solid dock, they nodded in assent.

"Our safety," I went on, "is to find a sheltered anchorage and ride this storm out with a good hold on the bottom."

With the several mooring lines recovered and taken aboard, *Skipper Sam II* responded to her reverse gears and backed away. We started for Loon Harbor, just a few minutes away. With daughter Cindy and Paul at work rigging the anchor, it was a good time to brief our now nervous crew on the values of the boater's friend, nylon anchor line.

DuPont publishes quite a book, detailing the ability of a nylon line to stretch a full 20 percent without failing. Thus a boat at anchor, with seven times the depth in anchor line length (boaters call this the "scope"), can ride out a blow with what could be described as a "shock absorber" holding her in place.

Rounding the entrance into Loon Harbor, one of the best hiding places on the north shore, we dropped the "hook" in the lee of the high forested bluff. Paul let the line run a bit and then took a turn on the bow cleat. Backing down, the boat caused the anchor to be "set" almost immediately, in 30 feet of water.

Continuing to back away, we let more than 200 feet of additional line slide into the water before Paul cinched it around the cleat on the bow. Large drops of rain accompanied the increasing gusts of wind.

Jan and our guests were busy closing windows, having already removed anything that might blow away from all exposed areas. She had gathered and stacked life jackets in the main cabin, handing one to each member of the crew.

Suddenly, silence.

The blow followed in but a moment. Tree branches emerged from the point just ahead of us, sailing high above the boat. The blinding flash of cloud-to-ground lightning was followed by almost instantaneous bursts of thunder, rattling the windows and echoing immediately from the nearby bluffs.

Shipper Sam II "heeled over" on her right side, swinging violently in the process. Like a tethered stallion she sought her freedom, adding tension to the anchor line, already bowstring tight.

The anchor held.

Blinding torrents of rain followed, obscuring vision in all directions. Our safety depended on a good Danforth 35H hi-tensile anchor and DuPont's best anchor line. The boat surged back and forth, coming to rest only as the wind died. The crew watched this display of nature's might in awed silence. Finally, it was over.

The anchor came aboard after quite a fight with a waterlogged tree it had found on the bottom of the harbor. We coiled the line and stowed all the tackle. Under way again, we passed the tiny cove.

No trace was evident of any form of dock where we had been moored, a scant hour before.

Originally appeared in Lake Superior Magazine, *August/September 1989*

The Queen of the Lakes

Captain Ray Lundquist watches with interest as the small bulldozer is lifted from the cargo compartment of his ship. The tedious unloading process is finally at an end. The taconite pellets have all been removed from the belly of the *Edward L. Ryerson*.

As the 'dozer assisted, the bridge crane unloaders performed well, one more time, just as they have since the 1930s. It has taken many precious hours, hours that are totally foreign to newer vessels or those that have been converted to self-unloading ships so common today.

Once the undisputed queen of the Great Lakes cargo haulers, the *Edward L. Ryerson* now has to compete for shipments destined for the few docks still able to unload the remaining "straight-deckers" like itself – boats unable to unload themselves.

Finally, the last truckload of iron ore pellets is en route to Blast Furnace Number 7 at Inland Steel's Indiana Harbor Works east of Chicago. Wasting no time, Lundquist calls for power as the mooring lines are recovered aboard. With the single long blast of the horn, the signal of a vessel getting under way, the *Ryerson* eases away from the dock.

Standing on her fog-shrouded deck, 730 feet from bow to stern, I watch the changing scene. As we move toward Lake Michigan, the whole Inland Steel complex passes through our

limited view, including the *Wilfred Sykes*, a converted self-unloader, and the 728-foot *Joseph Block*, Inland's newest vessel. Here the steels which become washing machines, automobiles, skyscrapers and bridges are born in the searing heat of the blast furnaces.

Once out in Lake Michigan, the comfortable routine of a voyage embraces our little group. Good company, excellent food and a chance to observe master mariners at work make such a trip so very special.

Capt. Lundquist makes a point. Less than 60 U.S. ships are still active in Great Lakes trade, a far cry from the more than 600 ships in service during World War II. Beginning in the 1950s, newer and larger vessels appeared, one boat often replacing five or six of the older fleet members. These new boats are remarkable not only for their length, often more than 700 feet, but for the giant turbine drive systems which dwarf anything seen in the past. Familiar names have adorned the bows of these vessels: *Edward B. Greene, Edmund Fitzgerald, Arthur M. Anderson, John Sherwin* and, in 1960, the queen of the lakes *Edward L. Ryerson*.

Named after their chairman, the *Edward L. Ryerson* embodies more foresight, quality and respect for her crews than had previously been seen on the Great Lakes. She is easily able to handle cargos of more than 25,000 tons, while speeding along in excess of 16 knots. But she cannot unload herself.

Dressing her functional red hull with the famous Inland white stripe was the final appointment, setting off her broad forward and after houses and large stainless steel stack.

There is no mistaking her, she is beautiful!

Self-unloaders were first thought to be bulky, inefficient ships, a necessary evil to be endured, servicing obscure ports that might need occasional cargos of stone or coal. Only after the closing of many steelmaking facilities, and the scrapping of their unloading machinery, did the logic of self-unloaders emerge.

As the Inland fleet changed, the *Wilfred Sykes* was converted to a self-unloader and several older boats were removed from service. The *Joseph L. Block*, a new-generation bulk carrier, was launched, able to unload herself anywhere! The *Ryerson* spent more and more time at an out-of-the-way dock at Indiana Harbor, her pilothouse shuttered, her decks silent. Offered for sale, no buyer could be found, even at the paltry figure of $1 million. Few places remained where she could unload.

From our foggy pilothouse perch, radar tells us we are approaching the north end of Lake Michigan. As we pass under the Mackinac Bridge, the mighty structure remains invisible in the

At Inland Steel's Indiana Harbor Works, the Edward L. Ryerson *has its load of taconite pellets removed for use in the making of steel in Inland's blast furnaces.* Lake Superior Magazine *photo.*

dense fog. The Grand Hotel of Mackinac Island, usually a remarkable sight, is hidden by the weather.

After a change of watch, more memories emerge from another deck officer. We are entering the St. Marys River, the twisting path to the locks and access to Lake Superior. The officer's point is simple: "America's steelmakers are improving their process and their products, and though much smaller than in the old days, the industry of today is world competitive."

In the Great Lakes basin alone, some 600 steelmaking or steel consuming facilities have been shuttered. Most have felt the impact of the wrecker's ball. It's a far cry from the respect they earned 50 years ago in giving us the means to win a world war. More than 30 percent of the steel made in the United States today comes from electric furnace "mini-mill" facilities, plants that consume scrap, not iron ore. For steel, the constant is change.

As we approach Sault Ste. Marie, the fog lifts, granting us a ringside seat as the deck crew prepares for locking through. Deck hands are swung out on a boom and lowered to the lock walls by means of a board "chair" on the end of a line. Soon we are secured, the lock doors close and the ascent begins. In almost no time we are again under way, and our companion fog reappears.

Once out into Whitefish Bay, our discussion resumes. The challenges are many, but we agree that America thrives on adversity.

Inland Steel says it is committed to surviving in this battle, joining with a Japanese steelmaker in a new plant to produce even finer grades of steel. The *Ryerson* brings a portion of the needed raw materials, still cost effective to a slight degree. To convert her to a self-unloader would require more than $15 million, money needed in many other sectors of Inland Steel. She presses resolutely on, her fate in doubt, her performance under constant scrutiny.

The next evening finds us at Taconite Harbor on Lake Superior's Minnesota north shore, concealed until the last minute by the ever-present fog. We linger on the ship during the loading, but, too soon, it is time to go ashore, our brief idyll over. We make our way along the dock toward our waiting car.

Turning around, I watch the loading of the last of the taconite cargo, noting how Captain Ray Lundquist gives orders to his crew as the *Edward L. Ryerson* gets under way once again. Little time has been wasted. In the glare of light, her stack stands out.

She is, I reflect, still most beautiful, still very much the Queen. In so many ways she stands for the best we can be as a society, a joining of strength, beauty, integrity and trust.

At a time when utility and cost pre-empts beauty, when boxlike deckhouses are the norm to save the expense of rolling plate, the *Ryerson* is almost an anachronism. To those of us who love the lakes, she is a proud beauty. To the flinty-eyed accountants who seem to make most of the decisions, she is short in the "return on investment" column.

Are we, as a country, really at the point we can turn our backs on the Queen? Will we somehow be better when she is but a memory?

Questions to ponder.

Originally appeared in Lake Superior Magazine, *October/November 1991*

Note: The *Ryerson* was put into mothballs in early 1994, but emerged to sail again in 1997 and 1998. She was laid up in 1999, with a decreased demand for domestic steel due to imports.

Lake Superior's Explorers, Wausau Contingent

The following piece was written several years before I made my first circumnavigation of Lake Superior and undoubtedly served as a spur to make my own trip.

Our Lake Superior attracts dreamers! The lure of the unknown, to follow the watery trail used by the earliest inhabitants attracts a fascinating group of people. Each drawn by a very private interpretation, an almost mystic lute.

In modern times, if you are a dentist with an itchy foot, you use long days in the office to plan excursions. If you have a friend who is one fine teacher, you plan your excursions in the summer framework.

If you live in Wausau, Wisconsin, Lake Superior can easily represent the ultimate challenge. And so it came about. Dr. Frederick Prehn and his lifelong sidekick, Dan Hagge, began to plan their ultimate adventure: to cruise around Lake Superior. Once the dream became a confirmed plan, with a date and time frame, the equipment list began to grow.

For an all-weather vehicle, they selected a Boston Whaler, an unsinkable, stable craft. Came next the engine, and its auxiliary, selected for reliability and raw power. Electronics followed, radar, Loran, good radios.

Immersed in details, the months flew past, summer approached. Test runs on local lakes proved the boat to exceed its promised performance; confidence bloomed. Launching from the Keweenaw Peninsula, Michigan, on July 6 seemed almost anticlimactic.

They headed west, at least briefly appalled by the magnitude of boundless water stretching ahead of them. The Apostle Islands were friendly, as were the surrounding communities. Again pushing to the southwest, the routine of confined life aboard a 21-foot vessel became almost normal.

After exploring Duluth, Minnesota, and Superior, Wisconsin, the Lake Superior north shore became just another challenge to their increasing skills. As their big-water expertise developed, the brute strength of the Whaler was seldom called upon, shelter replacing the need to challenge. Accustomed by now to the

The traveling duo spent much of their trip taking photographs from the inland sea, including this view of the shoreline along Pictured Rocks National Lakeshore in Michigan's Upper Peninsula. Dr. Frederick Prehn photo.

constantly available weather reports and accompanying forecasts, the pair planned each leg with careful study of the charts. These kids from Wausau were becoming seasoned Lake Superior boaters.

We met these characters in Thunder Bay, Ontario, Doctor Fred stretching out his hand in greeting with his inimitable smile. Dan is sort of the silent type, so our curiosity was spread between the two. We confess now to being a bit hesitant, since summer brings out quite a bunch of folk along the lakeshore who might be charitably described as "different" or, in reality, carrying what seems to be just a few bricks short of a full load. Years of experience dictate that one should step back for a moment of appraisal.

Turned out that Dan and Fred knew who we were, since they had tipped off *Lake Superior Magazine* about their plans months before. I must admit I was secretly pleased, since even a quick inspection of the Boston Whaler revealed that there was absolutely NO WAY sails could be rigged on this craft. Being a power boater myself, these fellows, I concluded, must be okay! After close inspection, I was quick to praise their selection of good dependable equipment for both navigation and safety.

We headed north, Fred and Dan going their way, we following ours, promising to watch for each other. With a weather change in prospect, we sought the safety of CPR Slip, or Squaw Harbour as it is also known. This tiny sheltered bay on St. Ignace Island earned its name as a fishing hideaway by the Canadian Pacific Railway early in this century. The railroad maintained a hotel in Nipigon and cabins for company guests who enjoyed the abundant fishing.

As we rounded the last gravel bar, the first vessel visible was the Boston Whaler, Dan's cheerful wave a pleasant greeting. My respect for their evolving boating skills gained another notch. Many boaters have discovered to their sorrow that it is almost easier to walk into this harbor than to take a boat.

As we left for Rossport, Ontario, Fred and Dan set out to explore nearby Talbot Island, intent on following a dusty story of a lighthouse once being erected there. We didn't see them again until the big dock at Rossport, due mainly to an almost impenetrable fog. From there, they zipped off for a day of fishing the shallow banks of Superior Shoals, some 60 miles out, almost in the middle of Lake Superior. Returning with three incredible trout, proudly displayed, we started the grill.

"Wait a minute," I confessed to *Skipper Sam*'s crew. "I've been monkeying around this overgrown puddle of Lake Superior for 40 years, and I've never been to Superior Shoal."

Dr. Frederick Prehn and Dan Hagge of Wausau, Wisconsin, took on Lake Superior in a 21-foot Boston Whaler. Here they rest on the Grand Portage dock. Dr. Frederick Prehn photo.

Okay Fred and Dan – respect up one more notch!

We started out for the Slate Islands, some 25 miles east and 10 miles offshore in Lake Superior. Waving good-bye, Fred promised they would see us there. The 25-mile run would complete our 1992 outbound leg.

Their course was yet to cover hundreds of miles of remote and hostile shore before they found the security of Sault Ste. Marie. Weather and numerous adventures awaited them, challenges would abound.

They did indeed complete a circumnavigation of the lake. In the process they made a host of new friends, and when they loaded the Whaler on their trailer on July 29, it was with genuine regret.

Through their efforts and reports, more people than ever now hold our lake in both awe and profound respect. What fun to describe their trip as a "win-win" adventure!

Dreams DO come true, don't they?

Originally appeared in Lake Superior Magazine, *December/January 1993*

CHAPTER SIX

Mr. Harkness Had a Yacht

The Sinking of the Luxury Yacht *Gunilda*

The following is a two-part treatment of what is likely Lake Superior's most glamorous shipwreck. "The rest of the story" follows.

The long motor car, driven by a uniformed chauffeur, turned off the avenue toward the docks with a distasteful air. As it wended its way over rough and unfamiliar terrain, odors ranging from manure to tarred hemp assailed its occupants.

Coming to a stop almost at the gangway of the huge yacht, the chauffeur alighted carefully, watching where he put his highly polished foot. With a bow and flourish, he opened the passenger compartment door.

Dressed in crisp white slacks and a double-breasted black jacket, William Lamon Harkness stepped out, turning to assist his wife. The Hardings followed, joining in the ascent to the main deck.

Under the canvas overheads, greetings and introductions were exchanged with the assembled ship's officers.

"Captain," said Harkness, "we are ready to sail."

"Yes sir," responded Captain Alex Corkum, turning as he spoke. "Single up all lines," he said to the mate. "Recover and stow the gangway."

Well-ordered activity spread across deck, as neatly dressed deck hands made the pleasure yacht *Gunilda* ready for departure.

The daily inspection of all brightwork – the exposed wooden surfaces – had been completed. Terse orders were documented by the boatswain, who also oversaw the curing of any visible defect.

In the beautiful salon, two stewards polished the sterling chafing and serving dishes, wrapping each in its velour pouch. The array of sterling flatware was mirrored in the deep varnish of the table as gloved hands returned the pieces to the velvet storage cases.

A quiet excitement engulfed the vessel, as whispered comments were followed by knowing nods of affirmation. Deep in the hull coal had been stored, lubricants stacked in orderly rows, spare parts carefully cataloged. After endless polishing, the brass rails, gauges and portholes in the engine room shone like mirrors.

Mrs. Harkness watched with fascination as the mate rang the engine telegraph through its quadrant, stopping the pointer at "aft one-third." Vibration was suddenly evident. The nearby dock and its collection of buildings began to recede from view.

As the skyline of New York merged into the smoky, dust-laden horizon, the Harknesses and their guests repaired to the salon for the noonday meal. The voyage was under way.

Even in the optimism of 1911, few people saw the need to own a 195-foot yacht. An owner, therefore, was entitled to a few idiosyncrasies. For William Harkness, a multimillionaire and haughty owner of the *Gunilda*, his forte seemed common to segments of all levels of society. He was so careful with his accumulated wealth that some thought him just plain cheap! His business acumen, coupled with family and business ties to John D. Rockefeller and Standard Oil, had generated incredible wealth.

Lloyds of London records indicate that *Gunilda* was built in Leith, Scotland, by the distinguished firm of Ramage and Ferguson from plans drawn by Cox and King. Completed in April 1897, it was, according to the New York newspapers, purchased by Harkness in 1904. *Gunilda* was actually 166.5 feet long at her waterline, the 195-foot length achieved by including her shear and the bowsprit. It was the first of the family fleet, which would later include the 215-foot *Agawa*, built in 1907 for C.W. Harkness, and the 239-foot *Wahiva*, owned by his brothers L.V. and H.S. Harkness, also built in 1907.

Though the Harkness family had long lived in Cleveland, the lovely yacht was enrolled in the New York Yacht Club and berthed in that city. The Harkness family changed residence in 1909, settling in New York.

In 1910, she had carried her owners and guests to Lake Superior, providing hay fever relief in the process. Now in 1911, Harkness, his wife, daughter and their maid, with Mr. and Mrs.

J.G. Harding and their two children as guests, planned a repeat of the trip.

While it was a voyage that would lead to an amazing denouement, the real story lies in the people who were on the stage during this drama. Who were they, and just what might have brought one of America's wealthiest families to this wild and barely charted corner of Lake Superior?

That story begins with an itinerant Presbyterian minister during the 1820s in America's growing east. Isaac Flagler outlived two wives; his third was the widow of a physician, David Harkness. Elizabeth Harkness Flagler came into the marriage accompanied by a son, Daniel Morrison Harkness. The couple moved to Hopewell, New York, where another son, Henry Morrison Flagler, was born on January 2, 1830.

Of such names is the history of our country inexorably woven. Henry Flagler went on to represent those farmers of central Ohio seeking to market their grain as a group, for much better prices, to the buyers located in Cleveland. With his half brother, Dan, Henry went into hardware and distilling, the latter then a reputable business as well as a good customer for grain.

While his various business ventures prospered, he made what would become an extremely valuable connection in Cleveland by selecting a commission agent to represent him. That agent was John Davison Rockefeller.

David Leon Chandler, considered Henry Flagler's finest biographer, talks in his book about just "who was where" in this time frame of the 1850s. Consider the following: Andrew Carnegie, destined to become the father of steelmaking, was 20 years old and working as a telegrapher for $35 a month. Thomas Edison, a boy of 8, was a pupil at Port Huron, Michigan. William McKinley, destined to become president, was a seminary student. Phillip Armour, destined to be meat packing king, was working as a miner in California. These were exciting times.

It was a combination of Rockefeller, Flagler and Harkness that recognized and capitalized upon the real value of that "gooey black stuff" surfacing and clogging the streams around Titusville, Pennsylvania. It was a Harkness loan that gave financial life to what was to become Standard Oil. And it was Henry Flagler who had the vision to build a railroad to Key West, Florida, aimed at being the closest American port to the easterly terminus of the Panama Canal.

From this foresight grew fortunes – and a country.

It might well be said that, while steam generated by coal

Gunilda *passes through the Sault Ste. Marie locks in 1911, just weeks before her demise on McGarvey Shoal at the top of Lake Superior. Rossport Inn Collection.*

propelled *Gunilda* toward Lake Superior, the real fuel was oil.

William Harkness was imperious and had inherited his airs from his father, Dan, brooking no insubordination from his crew of 20 and expecting no less than perfection.

Gunilda was a remarkable vessel. Her glistening white hull, embellished with golden scrollwork at her bows, enveloped a world of fine woodwork, accommodations easily fit for royalty and powerful machinery. In her living quarters reposed the finest of spirits, an abundance of sterling serving and tableware, rare books and *objets d'art*. Custom woven carpets covered all of the living space decks, while framed tapestries graced bulkheads and stairwells where their presence might enhance further the unmistakable signs of great wealth. Large refrigeration and pantry areas held an abundance of foodstuffs, aperitifs and condiments. In every sense of the word, *Gunilda* was a yacht.

Captain Alexander Corkum was confident it would be a routine voyage; stops along the way were limited to familiar ports, where he was known. Dealing with those who had made the fortunes was an accustomed and comfortable task, but his orders clearly stated accommodation of the second and third generations was to be the responsibility of his lesser officers.

Alex Corkum feared no man, except his vessel's owner, Harkness. It was probably this fear that later overrode his good sense, when he knew he was in unfamiliar water with less than good charts.

The beautiful yacht journeyed to the Great Lakes via the St. Lawrence River, from New York to Cleveland, Lake Huron and finally into Lake Superior. The Harkness children joined the yacht at Georgian Bay, shortly before *Gunilda* arrived at the Sault Ste. Marie locks, which was indeed an occasion.

On she traveled, across Lake Superior to Jackfish at the top of the lake. While coaling at the fishing station, high on Ontario's northeastern corner of the lake, Harkness inquired about sailing directions and courses for Rossport, some 25 miles ahead. His captain had suggested they retain a pilot for that leg of their trip. Though they had been to Rossport the previous summer, Corkum recalled the restricted waters between islands and the dreaded "Old Man's Hump" which the 1910 pilot had described.

Harry Legault, a fish boat owner, was contacted. He said he would guide them for $15 plus $10 for railroad fare, a sum Harkness termed "outrageous." The owner ordered Corkum to steam on, not knowing that the *Gunilda's* date with destiny was but hours away. Of far greater import to Mr. Harkness, we can assume, was the preservation of the $25 still in keeping in the captain's safe.

Imagine the gall of that lowly fisherman!

It was the fateful day. As the stately yacht backed away from the coaling station at Jackfish on August 21, 1911, a rising sun began to illuminate the early morning fog.

Gathering speed, *Gunilda* entered Schreiber Channel, all available hands as well as Harkness on the lookout for McGarvey Shoal. Identified on their chart as "rocks awash," or slightly visible, they were about to find the dreaded "Old Man's Hump."

There was no warning. The rumbling sound of iron and steel meeting unrelenting rock rose quickly to a cacophony of tumbling belongings, chinaware from the tables, books and lighting fixtures from secured positions. Kettles containing soup and other meal items cascaded from the stove top, hardly noting the steel rough-sea rails intended to contain them.

Captain Corkum found himself propelled forward, losing his balance as he grabbed the compass binnacle. Harkness fell, reaching, as he did so, for the children now almost flying by him. Screams of the crew members were followed by wide-eyed wonder. The bow of the *Gunilda*, they realized, was rising relentlessly from her usual level posture. It seemed she would never stop trying to become airborne.

Edith Harkness William Harkness

Rushing to the port side rail, Captain Corkum glared at the offending water surface, horror soon displacing anger. The rocky surface of McGarvey Shoal was clearly visible, just a few feet under the surface. From his lofty vantage point, rock seemed to be everywhere. None of it, his practiced seaman's eye noticed, was "awash."

The charts had been wrong. This was but the first of several "wrongs" which were gathering in the wings to act out their part in this drama.

Not realized at this moment was a sobering fact: the visible portion of McGarvey Shoal was the summit of a 300-foot sea mount, with an almost vertical unseen northern face just a few feet from the point where *Gunilda* "went on."

As the ship came to rest, the vibration of the massive engine died to the shrieking sound of venting steam. An almost eerie silence followed, as the enormity of the problem began to sink in. The beautiful yacht was stranded, helpless and in danger, hundreds of miles from help.

An inspection was conducted by the crew; it was soon determined the boat was intact and had not been holed. In fact, the routine of shipboard life, coupled with increasingly pleasant weather, led the owners and guests to enjoy lunch in the dining room prior to going for help.

Captain Corkum had directed the launching of one of the naphtha-powered small boats. Almost relieved to be doing something, the crew responded quickly and soon it was moored at the bottom of the ship's gangway ladder. Harkness began the long trip to Rossport to seek assistance, while Edith Harkness and the children and guests remained on the yacht. The grounding had attracted several local fishermen and one guided the stranded sailors to Rossport.

It is at this point the story wanders, and several sources over the years have claimed to be the factual record. Having been a sometimes unwilling participant in the dispersal of such data, I feel obligated to clearly define what I know to be, and what I think might be, the case.

It is known that Harkness telegraphed his insurers, the Johnson and Higgins Company of New York, who held *Gunilda*'s $100,000 insurance policy. For those who romantically feel the *Gunilda* journeyed to Lake Superior loaded to the waterline with jewelry, gold and silver, think back to your last vacation. Did you find yourself hauling all your most valuable possessions along? Neither did the Harknesses.

The insurers, practical men, contacted the only nearby salvage company, the James Whalen Salvage and Tug Company of Port Arthur, Ontario.

Captain Cornelius O. "Con" Flynn, one of Lake Superior's preeminent turn-of-the-century marine men, happened to be in Whalen's office when the message arrived. In later years his son, Paul, enjoyed relating his father's version of just what happened when the Whalen firm, which Paul always referred to as the "Thunder Bay Towing and Wrecking Company," got under way.

According to Paul, Con Flynn accompanied Whalen on his big tug *James Whalen*, which left for the scene towing Whalen's barge *Empire*. Passing between Bread Rock, another exceptionally dangerous shoal, and Copper Island, they entered Schreiber Channel. As the stranded *Gunilda* came into view, silence engulfed the tug's pilothouse. Checking down their speed, they were soon looking up at what Con Flynn described later as the "most beautiful wreck I have ever seen."

Many contemporary accounts of the salvage attempt allude to the planned sinking of the wreck, the better to get it to the same company's dry dock and further escalate an already outrageous salvage bill. These stories have one common source, Adolf King, a native of Rossport.

As a young man of 18, "Dolf" King was present at McGarvey Shoal, along with William Harkness, who had returned to witness the salvage attempt. King claimed Harkness was concerned about the intentions of the salvers to use the stranded *Gunilda* as a "make-work project."

120

The Harkness family enjoyed their lunch aboard their 190-foot yacht Gunilda *before seeking help from the salvagers. Although it seemed an easy task to remove her, the boat slipped to the side of "Old Man's Hump" and sank in 240 feet of Lake Superior. Oscar Anderson photo.*

King was later quoted, "Harkness was never so right in his life. They were a bunch of pirates."

Several years later King was employed by James Whalen Salvage, which had a monopoly on dry-dock facilities in the area. Again, later accounts quote King as saying the firm had a bad habit of hindering, rather than helping, troubled vessels. After an "unfortunate complication" during a salvage attempt, a vessel would sink and be in need of complete salvage operations and dry-dock repair.

As Robert Horton observes in his discourse on *Gunilda*, "If the salvage company had unorthodox intentions, in regards to *Gunilda*, they really outdid themselves."

The first argument of record was the statement made by Whalen after a thorough inspection of the site. He wanted to go back to the Lakehead and get another barge, so he could place one on each side of *Gunilda*'s stern. He would then run cables under her, secured to each barge, to provide needed buoyancy while he was pulling the vessel off the shoal.

"You're just trying to get me for another towing job," Harkness is quoted as saying. "She went on there by herself, and she'll come off there by herself."

The adversarial nature of the project was developing nicely.

121

Gunilda, *shown in the early 1900s, was perhaps the finest sailing yacht ever to ply the waters of Lake Superior. Joe Schneeweis Collection.*

Paul Flynn repeated his dad's description of this event often, and it has appeared in other accounts. According to Flynn, Whalen repeatedly tried to explain that he could not take a "straight back" pull on the yacht because of the shallow water behind the vessel. He feared, Flynn recalled, that the necessary towing angle would destabilize the stranded vessel. He pleaded for the second barge, but Harkness was adamant.

Flynn watched Whalen get out a piece of paper and begin to write. What he created was an agreement to be signed by Harkness. *Gunilda's* portholes, hatchways and doors were to be sealed before the towing attempt would be tried. Even with this, Harkness would agree that loss of the vessel was not the responsibility of Whalen's firm. After a cursory reading, Harkness signed.

A 12-inch hawser was strung around both sides of the vessel and secured to the front. The *James Whalen's* steel towing cable was secured to the hawser while two additional lines were made fast between the yacht and the tug.

Flynn recalls his father describing Jim Whalen's orders, stationing men on the tug's fantail with axes, ordered to cut the towlines and cables if necessary.

Now let us turn to the October 1911 "Marine Report" for the next segment of our story. As quoted in Bob Horton's discourse, it explains what happened:

"An attempt was made to pull the vessel astern without success, but the *Gunilda's* stern swung somewhat to port. When the lines were readjusted and further effort was made to pull her astern, instead of leaving the reef, she listed heavily to starboard, submerging her house and filling her aft end with water.

"In about 15 minutes, it was observed that the extra weight aft was gradually lifting the bow into the air, and in a little while she slipped over the reef, stern first, and disappeared in 240 feet of water. All that was saved was the portable equipment on deck, which floated off as she went down, including naphtha launches, cutter, sailboat, dinghy and steamer chairs."

And there she lies today, in Lake Superior's darkness.

Later, as the party waited for the train which would take them back east to civilization, Harkness was overheard speaking to Captain Corkum.

"Don't worry about it, Captain," he said. "They're still building yachts."

Originally appeared in Lake Superior Magazine, *February/March 1990*

Next, I'll tell the continuing story of attempts to salvage or at least visit the wreck.

Shipwreck *Gunilda* Sails the Bottom

Remember? The glass was all that stood between you and the glistening jewel in the display window. As a little child, your nose was likely pressed against the transparent pane, want and jealousy fighting an unending battle in your mind.

Since it slipped out of the salvers' grasp in 1911, the jewel that was once William L. Harkness' yacht *Gunilda*, has lain in the darkness and sediments of Schreiber Channel near Rossport, Ontario, enticing divers who imagine her lying there under 240 feet of clear, cold water in the same way that the jewel in the display window lures the kid.

Gunilda was on its second voyage into Lake Superior waters in August 1911, when she met her untimely end.

After the stranding, Harkness, Captain Corkum and some crew members traveled by gasoline powered launch to Rossport, accompanied by a fisherman who had seen their plight and come to offer his assistance. Edith Harkness and the children and guests remained on the yacht.

As the launch left the Rossport dock on its return trip to *Gunilda*, Harkness and the others walked to the Rossport Inn. The old hotel, built adjacent to the railroad tracks some years before, had hosted hundreds of weary travelers. Though most had a story to tell, many of real interest, none had recounted such a shipwreck.

Proprietor Oscar Anderson listened to their tale with an air of wonder, promising to get them on the next train west. Hot food was wolfed down, the stress of the whole day now taking its toll.

Dozing in the tiny alcove of the entrance, it seemed just moments before the mournful whistle of the approaching train roused them. Boarding, they settled back to sleep for the long ride to Port Arthur, Ontario.

No doubt the captain and Harkness both relived with shivers those first few moments when their efforts were solely devoted to protecting the Harkness children on the bridge as the yacht, scraping and vibrating, rode bow-first up the shoal and came to a shuddering halt. The shoal was painfully visible along the port or left side. The

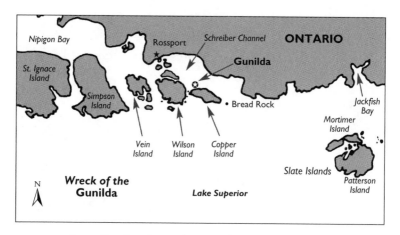

Nipigon Bay

Rossport

Schreiber Channel **ONTARIO**

St. Ignace
Island

Gunilda

Simpson
Island

• Bread Rock

Jackfish
Bay

Vein
Island

Wilson
Island

Copper
Island

Mortimer
Island

Slate Islands

Patterson
Island

N

**Wreck of the
Gunilda**

Lake Superior

water was but a few feet deep wherever they looked. To the starboard, only the bluish-black of deep Lake Superior could be seen.

Meanwhile, shrouded in darkness, the lights of the *Gunilda* welcomed the launch back from its trip. It was decided the next trip to Rossport could wait until morning, and all aboard settled down for a "fitful, restless sleep."

Next day, Harkness and Captain Corkum arrived at the Canadian Towing and Wrecking Company in Port Arthur. Captain James Whalen listened to their story, found the owner credit-worthy and called for steam to be raised on the big tug *James C. Whalen.*

With heavy lines aboard, extra provisions stowed and coal added to the bunkers, an even heavier line, normally reserved for towing the largest ships, was manhandled aboard and coiled on the stern deck as an afterthought. Totally familiar with the ships of commerce, Captain Whalen was eager to see this stranger to his waters, a 195-foot millionaire's yacht.

Arriving on the scene, Whalen was immediately concerned for the yacht's safety. For a short period during the salvage effort, *Gunilda* would be almost unsupported, either by rock or water. Explaining this to Harkness, he said they should sling the stern between two barges before they began pulling. In response, Harkness told him, "She went on there by herself, she'll come off by herself."

Taking a strain on *Gunilda*, the big tug couldn't pull directly aft because of the reef. As the yacht began to move astern, she heeled over and almost immediately began filling with water. Still partially trapped on the reef, she settled on her side, plainly starting a plunge to the bottom.

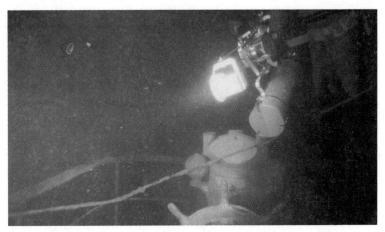

The wheel and compass of the luxury yacht Gunilda *have been well preserved by Lake Superior's icy waters. Joe Schneeweis photo.*

Whalen roared a command to the men he had stationed with axes near the tow line. "Cut her loose," he shouted. "CUT HER LOOSE – NOW."

Harkness, standing by in his launch, stared at the dying yacht in disbelief. Totally unaccustomed to anything thwarting his desire or command, he was speechless.

No longer fettered by the towline, *Gunilda* settled further, gradually righting herself as she began her sternward plunge to the bottom, some 240 feet below. Last seen was her forward mast and rigging, which disappeared in the boiling turbulence and bubbles that marked her death. Except for the panting of the tug's steam boiler, an almost unholy silence settled over the scene. No one spoke. The gathering of fishermen and their families, a few tourists and the Andersons from the Rossport Inn gradually dispersed.

The Harkness family and guests left on an early train, with William's last overheard remark to Captain Corkum: "Don't worry about it, Captain," he said. "They're still building yachts."

Salvage attempts were discussed several times over the ensuing years, but gradually *Gunilda* receded in the memories of most who had witnessed her passing.

But, in her own way, *Gunilda* had a guardian.

Dolf King, who had witnessed her sink and later worked for the towing company, told her story to a newly arrived Rossport schoolteacher, Ray Kenney. The year was 1930, and, over the ensuing years, Kenney discussed the missing yacht with others, knowing only in general terms her location.

In the early 1960s, King related the story to a commercial diver named Jack Coughlin, a resident of Port Arthur. This resulted in what we believe to be the first dive on *Gunilda* in 1960.

Kenney, who operated a charter fishing boat when not educating the local small fry, took King and Coughlin out to McGarvey Shoal. Moored to "Old Man's Hump," Coughlin went into the water after telling King how long he planned to be down. King, holding his safety line, studied his watch.

"Thirty seconds left," he told Kenney "If [he] doesn't start back up by then, we're going to pull him up."

After a moment the line slackened, the diver began his ascent. Almost delirious from excessive nitrogen, Coughlin claimed he had touched the mast. As they returned to Rossport, he gradually recovered, but Coughlin never went back to *Gunilda*.

The first real effort to recover her began in 1966. Ed Flatt, a 72-year-old retired railroader from Port Arthur, arrived on the scene. It was his intent to expend his modest fortune, if necessary, to recover the still pristine shipwreck.

With his young and enthusiastic wife he outlined his plans during a visit to Duluth, Minnesota, that year. A group, including this author, had gained some notoriety trying to salvage the sunken steamer *America* at Isle Royale in 1965 and 1966, and Flatt had followed our progress – or lack of it.

He was convinced that *Gunilda* lay in a sort of trench that gradually sloped upward toward Copper Island. Though he had never seen the wreck, he reasoned he could, with giant grappling hooks, snag the anchors or the anchor chains on the forward deck. Once this connection was secure, he surmised, it would be a simple matter to drag the ship up the trench to shallow water, where she could easily be salvaged. He acknowledged that a cliff existed in about 50 feet of water that would preclude dragging the ship to the surface, but this was a small matter for Flatt.

As the conversation over dinner flowed, I learned more about this fascinating man. He had been a volunteer on the tug *James C. Whalen* in the winter of 1933, when the tug searched the north side of Isle Royale for the missing steamer *Kamloops* and its survivors. He admitted that they didn't enter Todd Harbor, for fear of reefs and ice, but sounded their whistle almost constantly. To those survivors freezing to death in that bay, the sound of whistles must have been ironically sad. What, after all, could they have used to reply or gain attention? Certainly not the "Lifesaver" candy found among their remains the next spring.

During a dangerous deep dive on the wreck, this diver inspects Gunilda's *aftercabins below the top deck. Joe Schneeweis photo.*

I asked Flatt how he expected to "drag" a vessel almost 200 feet long up this long ramp. With sparkling eyes and boyish enthusiasm he explained his method.

"I'm in Duluth," he said,"on my way to Selkirk, Manitoba." He went on to explain that a large bascule or "tilting" bridge, spanning the Red River, was being removed. The giant bridge engine was soon to be his.

He was as good as his word. A few months later, he stopped again, this time with a giant truck and trailer and the engine. His enthusiasm hadn't flagged; success was imminent. In but a few weeks the engine would be set on a concrete bed on Copper Island, ready to pull *Gunilda* back to the sunshine that she had missed for 55 years.

The rest of the Ed Flatt story is hearsay, since my activities precluded a visit to Rossport in the summer of 1967.

He would call periodically, but his comments were decreasingly optimistic. He had rented a barge from Kimberly-Clark, on which he placed a camp trailer. He also had rented or leased a tug, which he used to try and snag *Gunilda*. He failed in this attempt, largely due to continuous bad weather which lasted most of the month. The divers he had hired played cards in the trailer, or remained ashore. It was Ed Flatt's last supreme effort.

Before we leave Ed Flatt, it is worthy to note he was, indeed, a railroad man. His thoughts were of pulling, rather than floating the wreck. We had suggested a number of methods of flotation, but his mind was made up. Finances, weather and advancing fall and winter conspired to terminate this salvage attempt. The severed bowsprit, forward mast and a light were all he could claim of the millionaire's yacht.

The other loser was the ship itself. In years to come, skilled divers would make their way to the lonely ship, finding torn and severed cables, broken windows and damaged brightwork, all mute testimony to the grappling hooks towed behind Ed Flatt's tug.

In the 1970s, two divers from Thunder Bay, Ontario, "King" Hague and Fred Broennle, in the company of Flatt, visited the site. The divers made three dives, one inadvertently to 280 feet, far below the intended depth. Only then did they begin to realize that Flatt might have ulterior motives.

Hague was an experienced diver, as was Broennle. After fruitless hours of grappling under Flatt's directions, Hague set off in another direction, his path evident from his exhaust bubbles. Flatt became very excited, realizing and later admitting his attempt to keep them away from the wreck had failed.

King Hague never came up, only his flashlight did. Broennle dressed to go after him, but the dive was in vain.

At the 70-foot shoulder on the reef face, he blew air into his inflatable life vest, striving to balance the compression of his diving suit. In his next conscious moments he realized that he had tumbled to the bottom, and he was lying under the bow of *Gunilda*.

His brain fogged by nitrogen narcosis, Broennle added a few breaths to the life vest, which aided his ascent. He ran out of air at 60 feet.

It was a limp and confused Fred Broennle that Flatt and Kenney dragged into their boat. A totally stricken Maria Hague, exchanging looks with Ray Kenney, realized that her husband was gone. It was time to raise the anchor and strike out for the security of the Rossport dock.

Seven years later, in a picture from Broennle's remote controlled camera, Hague's body was found on the bottom. It lay alongside the ship, totally intact. His remains were recovered, remarkably well preserved, mute testimony to the cold waters of deep Lake Superior.

The next group to become intrigued by the sunken yacht was a firm known as Verne Engineering, who had developed a submersible under a Navy contract. Their charge to develop a "Large Object Salvage System" resulted in another call to Ray Kenney.

One of the first pictures of Gunilda *on "Old Man's Hump" was shot by Oscar Anderson of Rossport, Ontario. Today the yacht resides under 240 feet of water.*

"We've got a submarine," Jim Leblanc told Kenney, "and we need your help towing it out to the *Gunilda* site."

With his partner Kevin Price, Leblanc and his submersible arrived in Rossport. To say it was the talk of the town would be an understatement. After launching the ungainly machine, Kenney began the tow to McGarvey Shoal.

As is often the case in such endeavors, Kenney watched more than a few bubbles rise from the submarine. They were followed by a quickly surfacing underwater vehicle, with two crewmen scrambling for the safety of Kenney's boat.

"Damn thing is leaking like a sieve," Leblanc said. "We almost lost her!"

The tow back to Rossport was with almost the same vigilance over the tow line that Jim Whalen had exercised many years before as he pulled *Gunilda* from the reef.

The enthusiasm of building the submersible, it turned out, had outstripped the need for inspection. The battery compartment had not been sealed against water pressure and this oversight almost added two more to the lonely watch crew on the sunken *Gunilda*.

After repairs, the submarine did visit the wreck, at least according to Leblanc and Price. No movies or photos were ever shared, nor are known to exist. Verne Engineering went on to greater glory in the oil fields, according to Kenney.

Next came a period during which skilled divers developed the equipment and diving disciplines necessary to visit and photograph the deep wreck. Gerry Buchanan, Ken Englebrecht, Dr. Joe

Schneeweis and Bob Horton, all from Minnesota, joined Canadians Fred Broennle and Ryan Leblanc in this organized diving program. All made several descents to the shadowy shipwreck, returning with the first underwater photos and movies of the yacht ever made.

A detailed description of these descents can be found in the "Deep Dive" chapter of our book, *Shipwrecks of Lake Superior*, from Lake Superior Port Cities Inc.

As each plan matured into an actual trip to Rossport, it was Ray Kenney and his trustworthy boat that counted. Loading tanks, gear and divers almost beyond measure, Ray took it all in stride.

"Wonderful people," he would recall in later years. "It was a privilege to work with them." Ray is easily the most colorful resident along the Rossport waterfront, a person well deserving the respect and admiration of all who know him.

Totally fascinated with *Gunilda*, Fred Broennle of Thunder Bay set out to purchase the wreck. He was finally successful, gaining title in the late 1970s. Broennle has expended several fortunes in his attempt to salvage and float his prize, but it remains on the bottom.

The Canadian government now disputes his claim of ownership, of course. For Fred Broennle, the challenge of weather and depth of water might become insignificant next to the ponderous bureaucracy with which he now must deal.

In summer 1989, two seasoned divers made several dives to the wreck. On the sixth dive, only one returned. Reg Barrett, of Toronto, experienced equipment problems leading to his death. His longtime diving partner, Fred Upton, was near him when he died, but was unaware of the problem.

Barrett was an incredible man. Among other accomplishments, he had made a successful swim across the English Channel. His death triggered a series of unusual happenings, the first of which occurred soon after several layers of Ontario government became involved.

The wreck was made "off limits" during the coroner's investigation. An underwater camera was brought to the site to assist in finding the body, but it became tangled in the wreck's rigging. A second camera, to help untangle the first one, soon also was fouled in the wreck. Despite great activity, little was actually being accomplished.

Two days later, Reg Barrett's body was found tied to the surface float above the wreck. With all the pontificating about rules, laws and other violations, the relief to Barrett's immediate family seemed lost in the shuffle. Upton later would admit he had recovered his friend by making a solitary night dive. Finding Barrett on the bow of the yacht, he had to hold him while making the several decompression stops on the way to the surface.

In summer 1990, Barrett's family spread his ashes over McGarvey Shoal.

Over the next two years, Terry Moore and Frank Fogarty, a diving team from Marquette, Michigan, made an incredible series of videotapes about the wreck. These quality underwater tapes, which include some interior scenes, may be viewed at the Rossport Inn. In 1998, the Canadian Film Board released a documentary about *Gunilda* and the ownership problems that continue to plague her.

The current owners of the Rossport Inn, Nedley and Shelagh Basher, have set up a display of *Gunilda* artifacts. The mast is preserved in the yard, with plaques explaining it to be a monument honoring both the ship and the men who have died while visiting her. Photographs and drawings grace the lobby and dining room, adding further explanation to the most unusual shipwreck on Lake Superior.

A few items, such as binoculars and lights, have been recovered from the wreck and are on display with Broennle's permission. Since but a few will ever see the wreck in person, travelers have expressed appreciation for Basher's efforts in explaining and preserving *Gunilda*'s memory.

While the good food and hospitality alone make a trip to Rossport worthwhile, to see and hear the story of Lake Superior's "Millionaire Shipwreck" makes it doubly worthwhile.

Whether the future will see another attempt to raise *Gunilda* from her watery grave remains to be seen. Disputes with the Canadian government over ownership may cloud the waters enough that another attempt is never made. However, even with permission, the mighty yacht may be reluctant to release itself from the hold of Lake Superior's cold depths.

Pause, as you study the foremast, now rising from the security of the Rossport Inn's front yard. Realize that for just a moment you are but inches from the object of dozens of men's searching, over dozens of years. Bodies now entombed or scattered over this fragment of a time long lost were no minor sacrifice. You are, fellow human being, on hallowed ground in a hallowed place!

Originally appeared in Lake Superior Magazine, *February/March 1991*

CHAPTER SEVEN

Favorite Wreck Stories

Benjamin Noble's Mystery Steams On

The Two Harbors, Minnesota, entry light just wasn't there. Several pairs of eyes peered through the rain-swept windshield, seeing only the glow of the ore docks. It was our first visit. We knew the long concrete breakwaters had an opening, but where was it?

Donning a rain slicker, Jim Bronikowski opened the forward hatch to better serve as a lookout. We started in, still unsure of where the entry was. We finally found it, and as we entered Jim pointed to the darkened stand where the light should have been. It was out.

Scared? You bet we were scared!

We had left Duluth, bound for Isle Royale, on the late September day in 1965. We acquired the old *Skipper Sam*, built in 1940, as part of our purchase of the sunken steamer *America*. All of this had followed my finding Captain Paul J. Flynn, hard-hat diver of renown, who had previously owned the Isle Royale wreck.

I couldn't help but think, as I probed for the darkened entry, of what a mystery such a port becomes when not lighted according to the chart.

Paul Flynn had only made a few passing remarks about a missing ship, the *Benjamin Noble*, which never did find this entry in 1914. As we gained the security of the harbor, my thoughts paused for only a moment on that lost ship. After all, *we* were safe!

Even now, more than 30 years after my adventure, or 85 years after the *Benjamin Noble*'s demise, that ship is still missing, and its

The location of Benjamin Noble *continues to elude searchers. Lake Superior Maritime Visitor Center photo.*

location has become a source of great interest to me and other shipwreck buffs.

Now wait a minute, you say. The *Benjamin Noble* still hasn't been found? After all, they found the *Titanic*, more than 2½ miles down in the ocean. And they found the *Central America*, loaded with gold, again more than a mile under water.

And the *Noble* is still missing? In this puddle we call Lake Superior?

Let's drift back to April 25, 1914. We're at the locks at Sault Ste. Marie, watching as an odd vessel approaches, upbound.

"She's just a canaller," you exclaim, describing her as a little 240-foot vessel more at home in the New York Barge Canal.

"Probably bringing coal to us here at the Soo," you say, "because she is far too loaded to go much farther."

Your point is well-founded. As the *Benjamin Noble* approaches the locks, several of the old hands marvel – her decks are awash and at sea level. Her obviously heavy load had actually been far greater when she left the lower lakes, and she'd burned quite a bit of coal since Detroit.

We catch just a glimpse of her skipper, 31-year-old Captain John Eisenhardt, as he positions her in the lock. We don't know he is on the first voyage of his first full command, and performing for us tourists is the furthest thing from his mind.

134

"He seems totally in command," you remark. I agree with you.

Only as the vessel leaves the lock, proceeding toward Whitefish Bay and Lake Superior, do we find ourselves speechless. Our eyes lock in undescribed terror. That boat – THAT BOAT – wallowing in the friendly seas of this confined waterway is going on to Lake Superior?

It happened that way. The *Noble* was committed to hauling a cargo of railroad rail to Duluth from Conneaut, Ohio. When her painted waterline had long since disappeared from overloading, a full car of rail remained on the dock. Eisenhardt was not happy, since they had agreed to haul the whole load in one trip. To take a second loading to complete the work meant they would lose, rather than profit, on the contract.

The *Noble* passed its annual federal inspection at Detroit, adding coal after the vessel had been declared seaworthy. Water freely passed over her decks, not an uncommon loading factor when she sailed the confined waters of the canals, but usually not even considered when travel on open lakes was required.

This visit to Lake Superior was not to be a normal trip, although the eastern half of the lake was benign and the Apostle Islands' friendly lights beckoned. It was only after rounding Devils Island on a course for Duluth that the extent of the growing weather disturbance became clear.

Heavy northeast seas soon attacked the *Noble* from the stern. She tried to gain the security of Two Harbors. Some reports claim she tried to make Duluth, turning back to the open lake after discovering that a pier light was out. With the same credibility, others say she returned to Two Harbors twice, warned off each time with signals as she approached the breakwater, not the entry.

Somewhere off Two Harbors on that night of April 27, 1914, the *Benjamin Noble* foundered and sank. She disappeared with all hands, allowing only tantalizing fragments of her to be found in succeeding days. A medicine chest was found at Lester River, on the eastern side of Duluth. Wooden hatch covers were found on Park Point, amidst bales of shingles discarded from another vessel fighting to save herself.

The *Benjamin Noble* is still missing, after all these years. This publisher still offers a $1,000 reward to the locator of her remains, but as yet no valid claim has been made.

Is this the year?

Originally appeared in Lake Superior Magazine, *August/September 1992*

The *Benjamin Noble* Trial

From the *Lake Superior Newsletter:*

Over the years, a whole collection of stories has grown up around this now almost legendary disaster. A medicine chest was found on the beach at Lester Park, in eastern Duluth. Several people of good repute have faithfully repeated their varied experiences of seeing the *Noble* off the mouth of the Amnicon River just through the ice, just east of the Superior, Wisconsin, entry or just off shore at the Duluth Pumping Station.

The newspapers carried the story of a little girl watching from her bedroom window that night, witnessing a vessel foundering and its lights going out just off eastern Duluth. Another dimension to the tantalizing mystery: Where is the *Benjamin Noble?*

In the 1950s, a lady saw a "vision" in the fog just southwest of Knife Island, 17 miles east of Duluth, which was so clear she could read the name *Benjamin Noble* painted in black letters on the white bow. She said she had never even heard of the lost boat, saying she was a clairvoyant and such visions were a common occurrence for her.

Her name was Irene Flynn and her husband was, at the time, engaged in underwater supervision of the breakwater construction at Taconite Harbor. Paul Flynn was one of the two most prominent hard hat divers on Lake Superior. Irene was a schoolteacher.

Don Van Nispen, a diving shop owner in Duluth, enjoys telling young scuba divers that he not only knows where the *Benjamin Noble* is, he has a magnet on the wreck. I know for a fact the magnet is on SOMETHING, since I was with him when we went to check out Irene Flynn's story. It's a big fat horseshoe magnet, war surplus from a radar set and should still have a hundred plus feet of red and white water ski poly line on it. When it suddenly pulled the line literally out of my hand, either as it grabbed or snagged, I looked at the depth finder. We were southwest of Knife Island in more than 150 feet of water. We couldn't recover the magnet, breaking the line as we tried.

At the risk of being a bit melodramatic, let's build this scene in our mind's eye. Come with me now to the bridge of the *Benjamin Noble*. You are Captain John Eisenhardt, this is your first command, you are in trouble. The normally hardly rippled waters of the eastern canals are nowhere to be seen. In their place around your vessel are insane, wind-driven waves, cresting with boiling white mantles, hesitating for but a moment before they crash with carefree abandon on the deck of your boat.

You feel the shuddering impact, even here in the pilothouse.

It's been a long night. You've been without sleep for longer than you can remember, your gaunt reddened eyes peer into the darkness as your wheelsman tries to follow your commands. The mate lounges in a long-legged chair, the chart and the navigation scales and triangles before him.

How many hours have you been up? You can't even remember. You knew command would be tough, but this is what you prepared for all your adult life. You studied her decks at the Soo, still almost awash. Despite the coal burned in passage, you still have a heavily laden vessel.

The danger signals at Two Harbors, where you sought refuge but turned in response to the warnings, have left you confused. What was wrong? Another study of the chart fails to yield answers – what don't you know?

Oh, how hard the turning away was – on the boat, the trust of your crew and your officers begins to fade. A sustained beam sea can destroy your ship and your crew, and the heavy vibration of the last turn into the wind has aroused even the most fatigued aboard. With resolute determination, you call for a course for Duluth, just as the overwhelming sea crashes aboard from behind the ship.

Everything seems to stop – as if in a movie with a broken filmstrip. You feel the ship settle, almost a resigned movement, as you rush to the back windows of the pilothouse. The deck is nowhere to be seen, even in the scant illumination of the after range light.

In its place is a series of marching whitecapped waves, marching with triumph over the vessel which they will soon claim. Before your very eyes a crazed surge of water breaks the windows of the pilothouse, pouring with joyous abandon into the room, followed by another, even larger wave.

This time the chart table gives way, knocking the mate down as he tries to fasten his cork-filled life jacket. As the wheelsman reaches for him, another wave comes aboard, rushing for the small stairwell to the quarters below. The last you remember is the dim lights being extinguished, your fear of failure being displaced by the gradual acceptance of your inability to breathe with lungs filling with water. Darkness.

And so we leave the *Benjamin Noble* to her world of perpetual darkness, a silent world, a dead world.

Okay, back to the story. Following the loss of the ship, the owners of the rail cargo sued the vessel owners. They won the initial suit, but it was immediately appealed.

Thom Holden of the Lake Superior Maritime Visitor Center in Duluth, Minnesota, has been able to obtain a copy of the court proceedings of 1915, which we've digested. It is reasonably apparent the *Benjamin Noble* is not far off Two Harbors, but probably in as much as 600 feet of water.

The last testimony in the trial was that of Captain William Rinn, 36-year-old master of the steamer *Lambert,* another 240-foot canaller. Not part of the original group of witnesses, he had been located and summoned. This is the first real look at the weather conditions at Duluth that night. From this testimony we can imagine what Capt. Eisenhardt faced in the darkness of the same night in his terribly overloaded *Benjamin Noble.*

Capt. Rinn took his loaded vessel out of the Duluth Entry at about 11:45 p.m. on the night of April 27. Let's join the testimony:

Attorney: What was the wind and weather at that time?
Rinn: The wind was northeast.
A: How about the weather?
R: Well there was quite a bad gale blowing when we left.
A: How much of a wind?
R: I should judge it would be around in the neighborhood of 25 or 30 miles-an-hour.
A: How was the sea at that time?
R: There was quite a big sea. It was what I would consider quite a heavy sea running when I left.

Here Capt. Rinn explains he set his course to go up the north shore, because of the weather, instead of taking the regular course for Devils Island.

A: Why?
R: I figured if the wind came more from the northward, I would be on the north shore.
A: Now, Captain, you later came back to Duluth?
R: Yes, sir.
A: What time did you get back to Duluth?
A. I got back about six o'clock in the morning.

A: That is the morning of the 28th?
R: Yes, sir, between five and six.

Here the witness is extensively questioned to verify he had not been coached on what to say, and had not given any other statement related to this lawsuit.

Originally appeared in Lake Superior Newsletter, *February/April 1992*

Requiem for a Lady

As you read this, winter conditions and the relentless pounding of our unforgiving lake extract the last vestiges of life from the 180-foot buoy tender *Mesquite*. Stranded on Keweenaw Point reef, she dies alone, an unwilling victim of the bureaucracy.

With highly skilled personnel ready to begin a salvage attempt, higher levels of authority hesitated, expending instead the few remaining hours available on the deployment of an oil spill containment boom.

Let's take a mythical voyage to the scene, trudging from Lac La Belle to the beach, dragging our inflatable boat. It is cold, but after climbing over the icy shelves, we manage to launch our Zodiac, and our reluctant little motor coughs to life with extremely limited enthusiasm. We'll follow the shore, dodging the occasional ice chunk, our course almost due east through the bay called Bete Grise.

The land slopes farther, the end of the eastern thrust of the Keweenaw Peninsula almost meeting the elevation of the lake.

The dejected vessel, listing heavily, comes into view. The lake is still and flat. It is an incredible, sad scene.

Thick ice covers most of the glistening black hull, which still wears its partially concealed angular red stripe. Painted service ribbons peek through wind-blown icicles high on the topsides. Remains of her mast, boom and cables hang dejectedly over her side.

A slight surge stirs the lifeless vessel; a creaking voice commands our attention:

"Who are you? What brings you here to my grave site, this forlorn and lonely bit of Lake Superior? In your little boat you could not have brought me help. Have you just come to torment me? Are you but more thieves and vandals, wresting more of me by day or in the dark of night?

"Have you come to still the echoes inside me – echoes of the days when life was put into me, not taken away? Let me tell you, dear visitor, I wasn't supposed to meet my end like this!

"It was Duluth, and a second great war raged. I was one of 46 buoy tenders built in that city. Our mission was critical: to outline and mark the safe channels, keep the ore moving to feed our steel

On December 7, 1989, just three days after grounding off Keweenaw Point, Mesquite had begun to deteriorate. Within two days, she was a complete loss. Frank Jennings, U.S. Coast Guard photo.

mills. Thus we got the better steel plate, the stronger machinery and the men with real know-how to rivet us together.

"After the war, we found ourselves breaking ice, setting and recovering buoys and supplying the dozens of lighthouse crews living a life of loneliness across the Great Lakes. Some of us went to salt water; one of us was there when the great bridge span fell into Tampa Bay. For more than 40 years we have cared for our fine crews.

"My sister, the *Woodrush*, gathered her crew in minutes – to respond to the loss of the *Edmund Fitzgerald*, setting out into a raging lake under the command of Captain Jimmie Hobaugh.

"My last voyage came as a surprise. We'd just finished picking up Lake Michigan's buoys, and I thought I was bound for Lake Huron.

"Another sister, the *Sundew*, was to be out of her repair status at Sturgeon Bay, Wisconsin, on November 20th. Based in Duluth, she was to pick up Lake Superior's four weather-reporting buoys on her way home, but her repairs were not complete and she was still in the shipyard.

"Thus, we were ordered to pick up the NOAA weather buoys around Lake Superior and take them to Duluth. We locked up onto the lake on Sunday, November 26, stopping at Marquette to pick up the lighted buoys. Then it was on to the Keweenaw Waterway, where we spent the next couple of days. From there we went to the Apostles, and then made a long run to the Slate Islands to recover a Canadian buoy, since the Canadian Coasties were on strike. Heavy

141

weather found us here, but after a bit of calming, Lt. Cmdr. J.R. Lynch, our skipper, set a course for the middle of the lake, where we recovered another NOAA buoy.

"Dusk had turned to night, the wind was east and we started for the eastern tip of the Keweenaw Peninsula, where a lone buoy marked the end of Keweenaw Point reef. In deteriorating weather, we found the buoy at about 2 a.m. It took several shotgun blasts to clear the ice from the lifting eye of the buoy so we could hook it, but we finally got it on deck.

"My fine crew had now been grappling, hooking and recovering buoys and their concrete sinkers for two solid weeks. Tough and miserable work, done exceedingly well. I guess they might have been tired, almost giddy from this weeklong race with the weather. They might have concentrated too much on recovering the buoy and too little on their changing position as I responded to the east wind. It was a slightly larger swell that set me on the first rock.

"I shuddered as the next sea put me on the rocky reef even farther. Screams and shouts mingled with alarms and the call of 'General Quarters' through my passageways. Unknown in the darkness was the extent of this wicked reef; it stretched almost a half mile out from the Keweenaw, barely under the water. Many of the rocks are house-sized, left by the scavenging glaciers 12,000 years ago.

"Another sea, another bone-jarring impact, bringing many to their knees as they fought fear and nausea. The constant pressure of the incoming seas set me farther on the reef.

"After an unsuccessful try at getting me off the rocks, my engine ran at idle for almost an hour, my last hour of warmth and light. Then incoming water flooded the engine room and it stopped, forever, at about 0330, December 4, 1989.

"Calls for help had been answered, and the *Mangal Desai*, a salt-water vessel from Bombay, India, responded. Her pilot, Superiorite Paul Halverson, and her crew performed a rescue mission which earned them a commendation. Dealing with wind, waves and shoaling waters, Halverson circled three times to recover my crew from our small boat.

"As the sun found my now lifeless deck, damages grew with each wave.

"In days gone by, skilled advice would have been sought, quick action and response would have been the keynote of all activity. Not so anymore. I was a proud ship, dying out there in the open lake, but no one cried 'save her.'

"On Tuesday, December 5, someone observed to the media, 'The vessel has barely five years of useful life left, anyhow.'

"Far from discussing salvage, they bustled far and wide to borrow and rig an oil spill containment boom. Oil, I could have told them, doesn't represent any great hazard in the temperatures found on Lake Superior in December.

"Extra anchors were the buzzword on Wednesday, December 6. Too much ice and too great seas again restrained salvage effort.

"A storm over the weekend of December 9 and 10 effectively destroyed me. The scavengers arrived soon afterwards.

"Now," says the tired voice, "hurry back to the safety of Lac La Belle. I'm not a ship anymore.

"I'm history."

Originally appeared in Lake Superior Magazine, *February/March 1990*

Farewell *Mesquite*

In the very early hours of December 4, 1989, near Keweenaw Point in Lake Superior, a tragic set of circumstances unfolded. The U.S. Coast Guard cutter *Mesquite*, assigned to Lake Michigan but on duty in Lake Superior to replace the cutter *Sundew*, which was in for repairs, had responded to an unusual request from the Canadian government to recover an expensive Canadian weather reporting buoy. The Canadian Coast Guard was on strike, and thus unable to perform the normal winter removal. The buoy, located near the Slate Islands, added several hundred miles to the *Mesquite*'s already extended schedule.

With the marine weather radio warning of impending bad weather, the officers of the *Mesquite* were pushed to tackle their next goals immediately – the recovery of a U.S. weather buoy in mid-lake and then a navigational buoy at Keweenaw Point.

The *Mesquite* headed south across the lake. By late afternoon, the U.S. weather buoy had been successfully lifted aboard the cutter. But by the time the vessel approached Keweenaw Point for its final pickup, there was total darkness. It would need to be an unusual nighttime buoy recovery, an action normally executed only in daylight.

The navigation buoy marked a shoal off the tip of Keweenaw Point. With seas and winds threatening to increase, at about 2 a.m. the buoy was hoisted aboard. While the crew concentrated on stowing the buoy, on the bridge Lieutenant Commander John Richard Lynch placed Ensign Susan Subocz in command of the vessel. He had been coaching Ensign Subocz on the approach to the buoy. After giving orders to depart the area, Lynch proceeded to his quarters by way of the mess deck.

During the period following the buoy recovery, the normally strict adherence to navigational rules seems to have been relaxed to the extent that no fixes were made by radar.

The officers had no knowledge that the vessel had drifted to a point north of the recovery position by nearly half a mile. When they finally got under way, their course took them directly into the shoal area of Keweenaw Point; the cutter ran aground on the same hazardous reef that had been marked by the buoy.

Through the winter of 1989-90, the Coast Guard cutter Mesquite *sat exposed on the shoal at Keweenaw Point. James E. Kliber photo.*

With the waves driving the vessel even farther onto the shoal, the crew of 53 began to lighten the ship as quickly as possible. They emptied some water tanks, and the recently recovered navigation buoy and its sinker were off-loaded. Two work boats aboard were launched. Well-rehearsed drills, very real this time, assured that the proper doors and hatches were secure.

After three hours of damage control work, water began appearing in several compartments, including the engine room. Orders were finally issued to launch the life rafts and prepare to abandon the 180-foot buoy tender. An Indian salt-water vessel, the *Mangal Desai*, had responded to a call for assistance, and its welcome lights could be seen to the northeast.

With the skilled assistance of Upper Great Lakes pilot Paul Halverson aboard the *Desai*, the *Mesquite's* crew was rescued during the next few hours. Halvorson maneuvered his vessel in wide circles just about a half mile from the stricken *Mesquite*. A Coast Guard helicopter transferred three slightly injured crewmen from the deck of the *Desai* to the Houghton, Michigan, hospital. The following morning, the rest of the crew arrived in Duluth, Minnesota, aboard the Indian ship.

Later, Capt. Halverson would receive the coveted John T. Saunders Memorial Award in recognition of his seamanship. Also commended were the Seaway Port Authority of Duluth, Great Lakes Tugs, North Star Marine, Guthrie-Hubner and the Upper Great Lakes Pilots Association for the waiving of all fees associated with docking the *Mangal Desai*, in honor of its dramatic role in the rescue of the crew.

An evaluation of the situation at Keweenaw Point began immediately. Captain Jimmie Hobaugh, Coast Guard Group Sault Ste. Marie and the on-scene commander, rapidly tried to assess the extent of damage.

Divers from DonJon Marine, skilled salvage masters from New York, found many bottom plates fractured. The damage did not follow seams or weldments, and the fractures seemed almost random, as if the steel were brittle. The center fuel tank was found to be ruptured and the engine room flooded. It was initially felt that the ship could be refloated safely, once fuels and much of the excess weight were removed. Plans were formulated to beach her, if necessary, in the sand of northern Keweenaw Bay.

The Canadian Coast Guard cutter *Samuel Risley*, whose crew had abandoned its strike to get the vessel under way, arrived on the scene from Thunder Bay. With their help, a floating pollution curtain was borrowed and brought to the scene.

Amongst veteran sailors, the cry arose: "To hell with the pollution curtain, get her off that exposed reef. Everyone had a plan to save the *Mesquite*, each born of that person's experience. Anxious eyes scanned the sky, attentive ears listened to the weather reports.

Capt. Hobaugh weighed his options. His technical people felt the ship could be lightered quickly, and he directed the fuel removal to begin at once. There were four large weather buoys on the *Mesquite* that had to be removed. In addition, the vessel had been at sea for some time, and her waste tanks were almost full. This considerable weight had to be removed before freezing. Plans were made that included patching the bottom damage as part of the recovery.

By then the Coast Guard cutters *Acacia*, *Katmai Bay* and *Mobile Bay* were either on scene or en route. On December 8, Mother Nature called the next turn of events.

The temperature dropped, the wind rose and dense snow squalls obliterated the whole wreck scene. Within hours, the *Mesquite* was attacked by vicious waves, some 10 feet high. The storm drove all but the *Acacia* into the refuge of Bete Grise Bay. The *Acacia* stood by her stricken sister through the whole blizzard, reporting periodically as the list increased and the mast and boom were carried away.

After the storm, divers assessed the additional damage. The list was 23 degrees to port (left) and the rudder had broken off. Dozens of bottom plates littered the rocky shoal, allowing examination of the deformed keel.

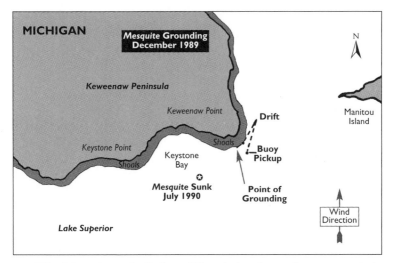

The *Mesquite* was badly hurt. The whole salvage plan was scuttled. Fuel removal continued, but Capt. Hobaugh had almost run out of options. Any further salvage effort needed to wait until spring.

Finally, orders came to administratively decommission the ship in January 1990 to allow the transfer of personnel and equipment to other Coast Guard units.

In the days and weeks to follow, the exchange of harsh words and charges rose to a fever pitch, as all sides of the issue sought to be heard. Hindsight remains 20/20, and in retrospect, many believe the ship might well have been saved.

The scuba diving fraternity was more than willing to write off the wreck. They began calling for her to be sunk in a newly created shipwreck "preserve." Since December 14, 1989, when newspapers had begun reporting the dual requests of the Alger Underwater Preserve and the Keweenaw Peninsula Chamber of Commerce, pressure for sinking the wreck had increased. Both wanted the *Mesquite* in their waters as an attraction for sport divers. The diving fraternity will treat her with the utmost respect, they claimed. She will always be remembered.

As a seasoned *Mesquite* class skipper, Capt. Hobaugh loved these sturdy boats that were built in Duluth during World War II. In November 1975, he had cleared the Duluth Harbor in command of the cutter *Woodrush*, *Mesquite*'s sister. In the midst of a terrible storm, they would be the first Coast Guard vessel on-scene at the grave of the *Edmund Fitzgerald*.

The decisions surrounding the disposition of the *Mesquite* were not easy for this man. A bid to cut the *Mesquite* up and deliver her for scrap exceeded $4 million. The cost of stripping usable equipment and sinking the remains in deep water was much less – about $1.5 million to $2 million.

The 46-year-old *Mesquite* had been slated for a complete refit the following summer, including new propulsion and electrical generating machinery. But the on-board engines "were just scrap value" equipment in Hobaugh's eyes. He directed the winches and electronics to be removed, along with other usable deck equipment.

In the spring of 1990, the captain reluctantly ordered the hulk prepared for removal from the reef. Hundreds of items, including clothing and equipment, would remain on the *Mesquite* when she was laid in her watery grave. To recover, catalog, transport and store these items for possible reissue would cost a small fortune. With the help of a huge barge, the vessel would be moved one last time. It was decided to sink it in 120 feet of water $1^1/_2$ miles from the grounding site in Keystone Bay. Here she could be visited safely by scuba divers.

She was laid to rest in July 1990. After checking the site for pollution, the Coast Guard left the scene. By agreement, the remains of the *Mesquite* now belong to the state of Michigan and its Keweenaw Underwater Preserve.

Hearings into the responsibility for the incident began immediately. Ensign Subocz, at the time the officer-of-the-deck, and Chief Warrant Officer James Thanasiu, the ship's engineering officer who stood accused of panicking during the period following the grounding, received reprimands during the disciplinary hearings. Ultimately, Lt. Cmdr. John Lynch's court martial found him guilty of negligently hazarding his vessel. He was found innocent of the more serious charge of dereliction of duty, which could have included dismissal and jail time. The judgment meant Lynch would lose seniority and not be promoted with the rest of his peer group. However, the verdict was appealed. The U.S. Court of Military Appeals agreed with Lynch and on May 31, 1994, set aside the court martial decision and returned the case to the Coast Guard for further action. As Lynch has since retired, no further action was taken.

Amongst scuba divers, wreck preservation is the current buzzword. Michigan has established whole underwater preserves, dedicated to this noble goal. Federal legislation further supports the aim of keeping wrecks complete for future generations. Only a few divers have complained about the increase in legislation and regulation, all aimed at preserving what remains of our underwater heritage.

DonJon Marine, salvage masters from New York, used a Weeks 297 salvage barge to move the Mesquite *1 ¹/₂ miles from Keweenaw Point to Keystone Bay. U.S. Coast Guard photo.*

With the *Mesquite*, the leaders promised, we'll prove a wreck can remain undisturbed by the new generation of enlightened scuba divers.

In the first hours of access to the wreck, divers reaffirmed what many of us have learned from experience. The majority of today's scuba divers are competent and a true credit to the sport. Their equipment is expensive, their use of it reflects the pride and skill they have worked to learn. Every sport, however, has a few really shallow and stupid participants, people who cannot see beyond their immediate gratification. In dive circles, the wreck is now known as the *"Mesquite* Mall."

Plundering of the wreck began immediately. Using pry bars, tire irons and hammers, the wreck is being reduced to empty and

With the ship resting in 120 feet of water, Lake Superior's cold waters will preserve this poignant reminder of the vessel's last hours. William Reynolds photo.

dark passages, devoid of any sign of its former life. The large majority of divers are dismayed.

In just a few weeks, this small segment of divers has set wreck preservation back a generation. Their conduct lends support to new laws that will soon threaten their sport. Because of their actions, the time is coming when all wrecks will be off limits.

The aftereffects of the night of December 4, 1989, continue to concern us. A good ship is gone, and her memory is being tarnished. It remains to be seen whether the public will do her memory justice. The consequences could be chilling.

Originally appeared in Lake Superior Magazine, *December/January 1991*

CHAPTER EIGHT

Even More Remarkable Friends

On the Coast Guard Cutter *Balsam*

'A what?" The friendly voice on the other end of the phone chuckled and repeated his opening remark.

"That's right," he said. "we sank a Japanese submarine with a buoy tender built in Duluth out in the Pacific."

His name is Vermont Johnson, he's retired and a longtime resident of Bayfield, Wisconsin. During World War II, he was chief boatswain's mate on the *Balsam*, the first of a line of fine seagoing vessels designed to perform a myriad of needed duties.

Zenith Dredge and Marine Iron and Shipbuilding Corp. of Duluth were awarded contracts, laying the keel of the first vessel on March 31, 1941.

Launched on April 15, 1942, as hull number "WLB 62," she was commissioned on October14,1942, as the *Balsam*, though in time she would become known as *The Mighty Bee*.

The tragic and – to quite a few people – unnecessary loss of the Coast Guard cutter *Mesquite* on the Keweenaw Peninsula of Lake Superior in early December 1989 aroused memories around the Great Lakes and beyond. Jogged back into focus were thoughts of countless days and nights on patrol on these fine ships, shared by enlisted men and officers alike.

Vermont Johnson acted on these thoughts, getting out snapshots now 50 years old. A sister to the ship that had taken care of him through the dangerous war years was dying out on the lake he has always loved. He said, "I was really shaken."

151

The gunnery officer (left) and executive officer of the Coast Guard cutter Balsam, *built in Duluth, Minnesota, proudly stand above a small symbol and flag representing the only submarine to be claimed by a cutter in World War II. Vermont Johnson Collection.*

Things that float had always fascinated Vermont, and it didn't take the Coast Guard long to discover that he not only knew boats and ships, but he took great pride in his skills. As chief boatswain's mate on the *Balsam*, Vermont translated the wishes of the officers on the bridge to positive action. As the war developed, it didn't take long for the *Balsam* to get into the thick of things.

The ship was assigned to the 5th Task Force of the 12th Naval District from 1942 to 1947. Beginning with action in the "Slot" at Guadalcanal and almost continuously through the invasion of Okinawa, *The Mighty Bee* distinguished herself.

Far too modest a man, Vermont was content to just make sure we knew that a Duluth-built ship had sunk a sub. It was necessary to dig back into history for the remainder of this tale.

Donald D. Morgan, a Coast Guard correspondent, depicted this vessel in a wartime dispatch, that begins with "Aboard a Coast Guard cutter somewhere in the South Pacific…"

He went on to describe the ship, "which for security reasons, we'll call *The Bee*. She'd probably fit into the hold of one of Uncle Sam's supercargo ships. Her bow is fairly blunt and pushes through the water like a fullback. Her middle purposely sinks in like a swaybacked nag. Her guns would produce but token resistance to most attack ships. She's an AGL – a buoy tender."

Morgan pointed out that she was so small that the Japanese probably wouldn't waste a torpedo on her, but at Espiritu Santu, in the New Hebrides, "she went through six Japanese bombing raids. They didn't even come close.'"

Like many of the smaller ships, the *Balsam* carried depth charges, but she also carried something special – two sets of four rockets near the bow, aimed almost vertically, nicknamed "Mousetraps." As they bore extremely powerful explosives, two keys were required to fire them, one carried by the captain. He could fire the missiles from the bridge, but only after the chief boatswain's mate had inserted his key in the weapons themselves. They exploded only upon contact with a target, so firing was considered almost a "black art."

In fact, as Vermont is quick to point out, such sophisticated weapons were looked upon with awe, since these ships were "poor country cousins" when it came to almost anything needed to fight the war.

The Coast Guard entered the war as distant relatives of the Navy, but since they were saving downed air crews, they were spun off to the Army Air Force, an organization even less capable of supplying their needs.

As the story unfolds, it is easy to visualize Lake Superior residents reading these words in the Ashland, Bayfield or Duluth papers. The strain of loved ones facing a hated enemy halfway around the world was ever-present, and bits of news were savored.

Let's rejoin correspondent Morgan in his tale:

"It was late in June, about noon. First chow was over, and the second gang of hungry Coast Guardsmen was ready to sit down. At his lookout station on the bridge, Liberate Fazziola, gunners mate second class from New York City, noticed something peculiar on the surface of the water several hundred yards away. He literally screwed his eyes into the binoculars. "Periscope!" he shouted.

"General quarters sounded almost before the echo of his shout subsided. Men like Bonifacio Pedroarena, a radio operator from San

The Coast Guard cutter Balsam *takes on supplies at Canton Island in the Mariana Islands, near Guam. Vermont Johnson Collection.*

Francisco, left roast beef and mashed potatoes and dashed for battle stations. Smiles changed to serious, hard-set features as men assumed Condition Red. Scared men? You said it! Men can be scared and brave at the same time. Ask any hero.

"Quickly the ship altered course and raced for the spot where the periscope had peaked the surface – like David charging after Goliath. The ship's skipper, Lt. Cmdr. L.P. Toolin of Boston, was certain of one thing. If they could get there with depth charges before the sub surfaced, they had a 50-50 chance. If not, they were outgunned and not fast enough to make a run for it. There wasn't much choice. The huge tanker they were trying to protect was floating dynamite. She carried high explosives and towed two barges filled with ammunition and high test gasoline.

"*The Bee,* full speed ahead, reached the spot as the Japanese sub crash dived. If she had tried to surface, the buoy tender's bow, husky enough for ice breaking, would have plowed into her. A pattern of depth charges splashed white foamy spray around the target area. The sea heaved as they exploded underwater. The plucky little fighting ship came about and once more pointed its bow at the target area. Sixteen Mousetraps zipped into the air. The dull thud of an explosion was heard.

"'We're hit,' someone yelled.

"'Hell no,' shouted Chief Boatswain's Mate Vermont Johnson, of Bayfield, Wisconsin, 'those are my Mousetraps.'

"Five of the Mousetraps had found their mark. In a short time the sea was covered with oil, debris and the flotsam and jetsam that once was part of Hirohito's raider.

"Today, on the starboard wing of the bridge, a submarine silhouette and a small Japanese flag proudly recall an incident in the life of a Coast Guard vessel that looks too little to fight – but isn't, by a long shot."

Many of the sister ships of the *Balsam* and the *Mesquite* have lived exciting lives, but Vermont Johnson and *The Mighty Bee,* which began its life in Lake Superior, can claim this singular honor of sinking a submarine.

Originally appeared in Lake Superior Magazine, *October/November 1990*

The Islands Win, For a Change

"The Islands … are one of the best kept natural secrets in Lake Superior." So went a story by Larry Sanders, in his syndicated column "Northern Insights." He was talking about Rossport, Ontario's offshore islands, and the tone of reverence expressed by this highly regarded journalist is well justified.

The better known Wilson, Copper, Channel and Vein islands provide shelter for numerous other smaller islands. Each is distinctive. Towering cliffs often blend into dense forest cover; pebbled beaches beckon the weary traveler. Long a target for development, the residents of Rossport, neighboring Pays Plat, Schreiber and Terrace Bay have jealously guarded their protecting sentinels.

Most North Americans have become accustomed to some form of government management of our non-residential land. Once such control passes into the hands of a bureaucracy, however, numerous problems arise almost immediately. Bureaucrats, most people soon discover, see their role as "protectors" or "keepers of the faith," usually with little regard for those who pay their wages.

Rossport set out to challenge such a management plan, aligning forces within the communities that had disagreed with each other for generations. The Pays Plat First Nations Band Council saw the logic of this united approach and joined their neighbors in a series of meetings over several years.

The people won! What they created was a citizens board. Larry Sanders points out that it might well become the "Rossport Islands Citizen Management Board," or something similar. What is different – a whole new approach – is that the board is in control and civil servants will be advisors. For the first time, the power relationship between bureaucrats and citizens will be reversed, Sanders observes.

It took two years of lobbying, workshops and countless meetings, but Ray Kenney, Rossport's best known charter fisherman, feels it was worth it. Ray, the longtime Rossport school superintendent, has fished around these islands for more than 50 years, sharing their beauty with many a famous personage.

Let's take a good look at these almost unknown Rossport Islands. As a glance at the accompanying chart will show, we are

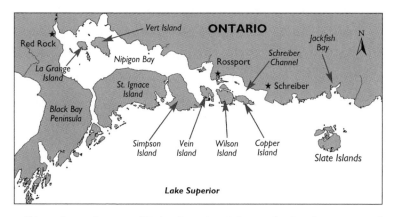

talking about the top of Lake Superior. Meteorologists have pointed
out that this part of the lake is subarctic, with all the problems of
such a hostile climate. Summer is known locally as an eight-week
period, preceded and followed by brilliant, shiny days. These are
interspersed between periods of dense fog and occasional dynamic
thunderstorms. This kaleidoscope of weather attracts true outdoor
folk, people of resilient strength, lovers of nature's beauty.

I'm fascinated by the exceptional populace that has chosen this
segment of Lake Superior shoreline as its home. Equally as interesting
are the travelers, those who elect to step off the train of life for a few
days in what can only be described as God's Country. Real people
find Rossport Country romantic, and the rewards are as diverse as
the personalities we encounter.

With passenger trains now but a memory, my reference to the
train of life must now allude to vehicular traffic on Trans-Canada
Highway 17. Few people sense the opportunity; most speed by. For
those with the good sense (and clothes) to linger, rewards abound.

Rossport is at once historic and contemporary, refreshingly new
and yet ageless. I'm no travel writer. If the john doesn't work, I'll say
so. But if I were, words could not adequately describe the
emotional reward of watching the play of sunset light over Rossport
Harbour. The thrill of standing in Ray Kenney's boat as a trophy
lake trout spits the barbless hook, its baleful glance almost a salute,
defies description.

Standing on the sacred beach of Cobinosh Island, south of
mysterious Copper Island, one feels attuned to the ghosts whose
presence is clearly felt. Even on the brightest day, something
compels conversation in a whisper, nervous glances seem the norm.
The beach is empty, the mysterious circular pits a curiosity, the lap
of small waves but a mild distraction. Still revered by the present

day Ojibway, Cobinosh has been a stopping place for travelers since the last glacier receded. As our boating friends have pointed out, the silence of Cobinosh – is deafening!

Approaching the Rossport Island group from the open lake involves steering for Battle Island Lighthouse. Visible for many miles, this beacon invites us to share one of the uniquely accessible areas of Lake Superior.

These are the islands that jealously guard the sunken *Gunilda*, a yacht whose story is recounted earlier in the pages of this book.

Take the time to visit Rossport. I won't promise good weather, or great fishing. I will promise good people, good food, more than adequate accommodations. And, even more important, a new respect for our incredible Lake Superior.

Originally appeared in Lake Superior Magazine, *April/May 1991*

Captain Horace H. Thompson, Master Diver

The shattering glass of his diving helmet faceplate occupied but a moment of his concentration. It was the jolt of darkly cold water rushing in, colliding with his suit's remaining air rushing out, that really got his attention.

He had collided with the rough bottom of the work scow following an uncontrolled ascent from the bottom of the Duluth (Minnesota) Ship Canal. The year was 1906.

Inhaling his last available breath, some air but mostly water, he gave three firm pulls on his air hose.

Standard gear for the underwater diver is a full diving suit with helmet. Marie Thompson Norick Collection.

Captain Horace H. Thompson prepared to work on the government pier in Grand Marais, Michigan, in 1910. He started his diving career in 1898. Marie Thompson Norick Collection.

The deflated suit, ruled now by his encircling weight belt, bore him back to the bottom of the canal. One final exhale, one solid gulp of water.

Darkness.

"Drowning," he said later, "is an easy death."

That day's task was not considered untypically dangerous. Working in 30 feet of water, Captain Horace H. Thompson was to install gas and water mains, connecting the city of Duluth with Park Point, across the bottom of the canal.

John B. Wanless, an early Duluth contractor, had hired Thompson for the underwater portion. Thompson was working off a scow, a floating rectangle of machinery and equipment, which was moored to the south pier.

Arriving at the bottom on that July morning, he found the currents strong and unsafe, rapidly shifting from one end of the canal to the other. Useful work was out of the question, and he asked to be pulled up, fearing that he would be swept away at any instant. At the same time, Thompson closed the air venting valve on the side of his helmet to make himself more buoyant. The trapped air quickly inflated his diving dress, causing a rapid ascent to the surface. The shifting current pulled him under the scow as he came up, and the inevitable collision took place.

The *Duluth News-Tribune* records his comments: "I attempted to stem the tide of water through the faceplate by covering it with my hand, but this was impossible. I then caught the last breath of air as the suit filled, and held my breath until I was almost bursting. I was compelled to give out and swallowed about a half-gallon of water. The sensation was horrible at first, and it seemed as if an hour of suffering had passed. Then I felt my senses going and seemed to pass into a pleasant dream.

"The next thing I knew they had me on the scow over a barrel and were jerking me upside down to bring out the water and let air into my lungs. Soon I recovered sufficiently to get home. I knocked off work for the rest of the day."

At the turn of the century, the Lake Superior country was holding a whole handful of economic aces. Sawmills whined and screamed into each night generating boatloads of lumber which built whole towns and cities. A red river of wealth, iron ore, clattered down the chutes into waiting ships. Elevators bursting with the grains of northern farms loaded countless ships. Men came to the lake for many reasons, but the predominant lure was age-old – money.

And the highest paying work, at $50 a day, was also the most dangerous – diving.

Those men who came to saw logs, mine ore and build cities had never heard of worker's compensation. If they affiliated with a fraternal order, however, they might be eligible to purchase a small amount of life insurance, regardless of the work they did ... unless their scribbled application listed their work as "sub-marine contracting." At this line a normally eager salesman would visibly pale and search the room for more likely prospects.

Thompson had earned the title "captain" honorably, and he was licensed to operate most Great Lakes vessels of the time. Born in Duluth in 1873, he worked on his father's tug for years before electing underwater work in 1898. The whole lake was a beehive of construction, and divers were in great demand. We accept the piers and docks of the lake almost without thought. Yet, it is worth considering the divers who labored in murky darkness to assure the structural integrity of where we casually stand.

Capt. Thompson's reputation was widely known, and in the ensuing years the demand for his services took him all over the United States. But it was Lake Superior that demanded most of his time. Following the great storm of 1905, he spent many years in the employ of the Pittsburgh Steamship Company salvaging or inspecting the wrecks of vessels now known mainly to scuba divers, the *Hesper, Edenborn, Crescent City, Hadley, Wilson, Cumberland* and *Lafayette* to name but a few.

His son John joined him in the profession, while another son, James, worked with them above surface as tender. Having a trusted surface crew is paramount in this treacherous work, and Capt. Thompson often arrived on a job, "just to watch," long after his last dive at age 70.

John and his daughter, Marie, carried on the work after Horace died in 1953. Marie went on to marry Jerry Norick, who is actively engaged in hard hat diving today.

Originally appeared in Lake Superior Magazine, *July/August 1988*

It Could Only Happen on Nights

While many of us have enjoyed watching the arrival and loading of the big ore freighters at Two Harbors, Minnesota, I'll bet I'm not the only person to wonder just who handles all of the details.

How come, I've wondered, the boat stops under that certain set of dock chutes? Why is the boat barely at rest before the ore or pellets begin to tumble into the waiting hold of the vessel? How does that train know which pockets in the dock are waiting for its cars of ore?

When I worked as a high school kid thawing ore cars and "punching ore," as we called it, I really didn't care. The money seemed incredibly good in those days, and it was always so cold we could pay attention only from one car to the next and wonder whether we could lift that iron bar one more time.

I learned quite a bit more when Jack Hedin walked into my office one day. Tall and angular, Jack retired after 38 years with the Duluth, Missabe & Iron Range Railroad, having held a number of clerk positions on both the Duluth and Two Harbors docks.

It's an intricate set of challenges that this job presents. Matching cars of ore from different mines – many carloads having different chemistries and owners – with boats of various sizes and owners, and distributing them through two sets of docks certainly involves considerable thought and planning. While computers have lightened the load considerably, time was when one train required at least six hours of a worker's undivided attention. Railroads needed great numbers of clerks to administer this work. And each car had to be billed separately.

Jack says this is now done by a computer in about 20 minutes. When asked about his work, he begins spinning yarns, and even has a name for his tales. Referring to the 24-hour nature of the job, with a laugh he'll say, "It could only happen on nights."

"The *William Clay Ford* had just cleared the Duluth Aerial Bridge on its way to the Duluth Docks," Jack says. "Captain Erickson called me at the docks to say there was quite a fire in West Duluth, which didn't seem to have any action around it. Had it been reported?

"I called the fire department and relayed the captain's message. No fire had been reported." The fire was quickly found and put out … directly across the street from the Piedmont Avenue fire hall."

As Jack points out, "It could only happen on nights."

Jack Hedin's grandfather was one of the first employees of the Duluth and Iron Range Railway, predecessor of the Duluth, Missabe & Iron Range Railroad. Gust Hedin's name is on the plaque near the original D&IR engine, the *3 Spot* in Two Harbors at the Lake County Historical Society Museum, which was formerly the D&IR depot. Jack is the last of 20 of Gust's relatives who have worked for the DM&IR or the original D&IR railroad. His mother's family homesteaded in the Lax Lake area north of Silver Bay. His grandmother was a Johnson, from the famous Isle Royale and north shore Johnson family.

Jack was always active in the union, sometimes almost to the complete frustration of management. He really got their attention, however, when he violently opposed the union imposing a "union shop" rule requiring all hourly employees to belong.

"If this happens," he pointed out, "it is the end of our union working for us!"

His reasoning was: "As long as membership was voluntary, the union would earn the members' support by looking out for their best interests. Once it was a rule, they would just collect dues."

Jack lost that battle, but says many of his fellow workers eventually found that he was right.

Another of Jack's tales: "The *Philip R. Clarke* was to arrive at the north side of Dock 1 in Two Harbors," Jack remembers. "The *Benjamin E. Fairless* was just finishing loading on that side of the dock, when I called the *Clarke*.

"'The *Fairless* has one or two pockets to go, but we could use an extra few minutes for clearing the harbor – could you slow down a little?'

"It was one of those beautiful nights on Lake Superior, so the captain just cut the power, and literally let the *Clarke* coast along on her own.

"Unfortunately, the last pocket for the *Fairless* ended up breaking the flat cable, the means used to raise and lower the loading spouts. There would be a delay of up to two hours.

"I again called the *Clarke*, advising them of the delay.

"Two hours later, the *Edna G.* (the historic steam powered company tug at Two Harbors) called the *Clarke*. He was pushing the *Fairless* out and would be ready for the *Clarke* in 10 minutes.

The Philip R. Clarke *loading taconite at the Two Harbors, Minnesota, ore docks.* Lake Superior Magazine *photo.*

"Later, the captain of the *Clarke* was in the dock office, signing his bill. He gave me this summary of the *Clarke*'s arrival:

"'I cut the power when you called me the first time. When you called me the second time, the *Clarke* was headed toward Duluth. When the *Edna G.* called the first time, we were headed for Port Wing, Wisconsin (directly away from Two Harbors). When she called again, ready to take us in tow for the dock, the *Clarke* had turned further and was directly between the pier lights, ready to come in. No one touched the wheel the whole time, until she was inside the breakwater.'

"I told the captain they pay him big money to steer the thing, and the ship knows its own way!

"His response was, 'Don't tell anybody.'"

It could only happen on nights.

Originally appeared in Lake Superior Magazine, *April/May 1989*

Jerry Siegel's Most Incredible Flying Machine

I scramble into the cockpit, kneeling carefully on the small portion of the wing designated to carry weight. Settling into one of the back seats, I ignore the seat belts, since we are only going to do a bit of high speed taxi work. No flight today, I think, as I examine the bold sign on the canopy which reads "EXPERIMENTAL."

Sitting just ahead of me is Jerry Siegel, pilot and builder of this fascinating aircraft. Passing a set of headphones back, he moves levers and switches with his other hand in a very professional manner. As I adjust the headset, I hear the distinctive whine of a real jet engine starting up. I suddenly realize the Allison jet-turbine is but a few inches behind me! The earphones relate Jerry's communication:

"Duluth Ground Control," he says, "this is experimental N1OJS at the North Country ramp, requesting permission to taxi to Runway 21 – for aircraft familiarization."

"Experimental 10JS, you are cleared to taxi to Runway 21," is the crisp reply.

Moving the throttle forward, Jerry releases the brakes and we are rolling. Glancing at the passing row of parked aircraft, I realize I am sitting in the only aircraft exactly like this one in THE WHOLE WORLD! Jerry Siegel built it from a collection of kit parts over the past five years. I am sitting in aviation history, a milestone!

Jerry Siegel is from Los Angeles, arriving in Duluth, Minnesota, when he and his father, Milton, purchased the Clyde Iron complex in 1987. Their business is major industrial equipment auctions and the Clyde Iron sale was to be but another feather in their cap. But tragedy struck with the untimely death of Jerry's father. While the sale was successful, Jerry elected to stay in Duluth and develop the growing Clyde Industrial Park.

His interest in aviation led to the purchase of a Cessna 152, which he based in Duluth.

"You Lake Superior folks," he loves to point out, "haven't a clue of how fortunate you are to live in what I now realize is paradise – at least in the summer!"

In 1987, Jerry learned that a partially assembled aircraft kit was available, a "Prescott Pusher." It was a fiberglass and aluminum

Jerry Siegel preparing his experimental plane for another flight. Lake Superior
Magazine *photo.*

fuselage, with retractable landing gear and a spacious four-seat
cockpit. Depending on what engine was installed, it could fly at
more than 250 mph.

When this aircraft flew for the first time on October 7, 1991,
Jerry, then 33 years old, had five years and a considerable amount
of money and time invested. It was worth it. Experimental N1OJS
reflects the leading edge of high efficiency personal aircraft design.

Design allowed for a conventional 300-horsepower engine.
This wasn't even a consideration for Jerry. He redesigned the engine
compartment to hold an Allison 250-C18-C-S jet turbine engine.
This well-proven power plant is found in jet helicopters, as it is far
more weight efficient than a conventional engine. All he had to do
now was tie a conventional propeller gearbox to this power source,
using short blades, since the propeller would be behind the plane.

I won't bore you with the details, but Jerry wound up putting
the engine in the bird upside down, requiring a complete redesign
of the lubrication system. He connected the propeller gear box with
a titanium shaft. All of this, while working very well, was far from
Federal Aviation Agency standards. While granting "Experimental"
status, they removed the product identity plate from the engine to
protect the manufacturer from liability.

All of the linkage in this totally unusual creation, by which the pilot tells the aircraft and its engine what to do, was designed and built by Jerry. Totally new instrumentation was required, including Collins radios, the Mercedes-Benz of aircraft communications.

Wow. Here I am, in a one-of-a-kind aircraft, built in Duluth! As an experimental airplane, Jerry could fly it solo, but with a passenger, he cannot leave the ground for the bird's first 40 hours of flight time. It is legal, however, to experience the raw power of a high speed taxi on an unused runway. After this exhilarating experience, we return to the ramp.

I want to know much more. Every one of us has created something special in our lives and, for Jerry Siegel, this must have been the highlight.

"Jerry," I ask, as we remove our headphones and climb down from the airplane, "how does it fly?"

With a reflective air, he pauses for a moment and then looks straight at me. "Jim," he says, "I gathered pieces and then assembled them. I redesigned and planned changes, estimated how they would affect aircraft weight and balance, always wondering how it would finally fly."

Excitement emerges, and he is again experiencing that first flight. Here is how it was:

With control tower approval, he taxis up and down the long Duluth runway, feeling the lightness of the craft as it approaches takeoff speed. Back to the hangar, another detailed inspection, everything again satisfactory. Adrenaline flowing, he forces himself to again review the whole project.

It's right, he thinks. *It's time to fly!*

"Duluth Tower, Experimental N10JS requests clearance to the runway – for additional performance testing."

The usually dispassionate response seems long in coming. Or is it just because he is totally wound-up?

"Experimental N1OJS, are you asking for taxi or takeoff clearance?"

"I'm not certain," Jerry responds. "I'll let you know."

Throttle forward, the engine noise and ground speed increases. Glancing across the instrument panel, he finds temperatures, oil pressure and vacuum in order. Glancing ahead, it seems the segments of the runway center line are passing under the nose with incredible speed! He pulls back on the control yoke, gently urging the nose up toward the environment to which it had been born. Vibration from the landing gear ceases, he glances to the side.

The runway is falling away beneath him. He gasps with a mixture of fear, excitement and sheer exultation.

"It flies!" he screams to an empty cockpit, thinking, *I built this airplane all by myself.* With another shout he cries, "IT FLIES!"

Alternating views of blue sky and green trees gain his attention. He is overcontrolling the airplane, he realizes, flying like over the humps on a camel. Letting go of all but a marshmallow touch control yoke, NlOJS – and its totally unglued pilot – settles down for its first flight.

Circling over the airport they soon are at 4,000 feet and the adrenaline rush subsides. Legs quit shaking, gentle adjustments to the flight path are tested.

"It flies," he repeats to himself, "now let's see if it lands."

"Duluth tower, N1OJS requests permission to land."

As he lines up with the runway, Jerry reduces power, suddenly realizing he is adjusting a jet engine for the first time in his flying career. Raising the nose, his speed decreases, allowing loss of altitude as he approaches the end of the long runway.

He is still marveling at the visibility the wide windshield provides as the wheels gently touch the runway. Lowering to the nose gear, N1OJS is almost docile as it slows. Turning off on a taxiway, the radio conveys congratulations from the tower.

Coming to a stop, Jerry opens the aircraft log. "October 7, 1991," he writes with shaking hand. "Duluth, MN, FIRST FLIGHT."

It is Jerry's dream to produce this unique aircraft in quantity, in Duluth. By building and selling it as a kit, to be assembled by the purchaser, the liability insurance costs are minimal.

Translating an idea into reality seems to be a fun challenge for Jerry Siegel. It's really just another dimension of the American dream, and those who know Jerry well feel the best is yet to come!

Originally appeared in Lake Superior Magazine, *December/January 1992*

A Lifetime of Royale Memories

As we negotiate the channel between the reefs stretching toward us from Barnum and Booth islands, we remember almost automatically that at least a part of their light color is the reflected glitter of many propeller blades.

Lying under the bluffs of much larger Washington Island, at the southwest end of Isle Royale, these two islands form a perfect sheltered harbor. Entering is a step back into life on Lake Superior as it used to be. Studying the bottom, we drop the hook in this tiny paradise, and time literally stops!

For the past few seasons this has been home for Enar and Betty Strom along with George and Elizabeth Barnum, who live a short distance away. They are among the fortunate few who can legally call Barnum Island their summer home. Their lifestyle is of the early years of this century: wood stove, bathing in the lake or washtub and the well-worn path to the outhouse.

George Barnum is able to conduct his hemisphere-wide business activity by radiotelephone, but this never takes precedence over firing up the sauna for all to enjoy. It is a magic scene, filled with breezes of varying temperature, an endless parade of changing sky and, of course, the ever restless lake.

Betty is the daughter of Arthur and Myrtle Sivertson, whose land was summarily pre-empted by the U.S. government upon the establishment of Isle Royale National Park in 1940. In lieu of monetary compensation of any real value, a life estate in the properties was granted to all those family members alive at that time.

Betty's grandfather, Sam Sivertson, came to Isle Royale from Norway in 1894. Sam's brother Andrew had come earlier, in 1892, and had built a small cabin on this very same island. By letter he told Sam of the opportunities available in America, and, in particular, at Isle Royale. "So like Norway," he wrote, "but we can own land here."

When Sam and Andrew arrived at the island by Mackinaw boat in 1894, it was the conclusion of a three-day voyage in wind and rain from Duluth. They were ordered off the little island by a man claiming to be the owner (he was), who waved a piece of paper which he claimed was his clear title.

Enar and Betty Strom have spent a lifetime visiting Isle Royale. They now live their summers in constant awe of Lake Superior's beauty and power. Lake Superior Magazine *photo.*

With his limited command of English, Andrew asked about the little cabin he had built. The man pointed to a pile of logs by the dock.

"I took it down," he said, "now take it with you."

Sam and Andrew spent the night with friends on adjacent Washington Island where they later settled.

Such was the beginning of the Sivertson families of Isle Royale. So many stories could be told, but the thread common to all of them is the constant involvement with the lake. Each day began with the trip to the nets, or, if the lake was too rough, never-ending repairs to the "rig," their fishing equipment.

After Enar and Betty's marriage, raising children became the focus. Isle Royale receded in importance, always just the familiar shadow on the horizon. Enar's skill in woodworking was devoted to maintaining the Sivertson Fisheries fleet, in addition to a full-time job at the Duluth Air Force Base. Time was found to build a lovely home on Pike Lake in Duluth.

Most visits to Isle Royale were more work than fun, since maintenance of the limited facilities fell to Enar. Betty's uncle, Stanley Sivertson, captain of the *Wenonah*, the boat that travels from Grand Portage to Isle Royale, always knew of one more project needing attention. Today, Art and Myrtle's home is but a memory. Just why it was burned by the National Park Service is unclear, and it is a less than pleasant subject, seldom discussed.

Following Enar's retirement, he and Betty at last had the time to do what they had dreamed and talked of. Her whole childhood had been summers at Isle Royale and, though they had visited each year, they wanted to go back without the constraint of limited time. The dream has now come true. They live in a small home which the Barnums and Betty's brother, Howard Silvertson, had kept intact over the years. She has even mastered the baking of peanut butter cookies in a wood stove oven! Some of the cookies, she admits, reflect their position on the pan, being closer to the heat source.

For a number of years, Betty has been writing a letter to her several children and grandchildren, describing what it was like to grow up on Isle Royale. It is filled with observations that remain almost childlike in clarity, despite the intervening years. She calls it "Isle Royale, From My Point of View." To Betty, the point of view is a real point, affording a view of the distant north shore in one direction and the ever-changing island scene on the other.

Here are her roots; the well-worn paths are those traveled by her family since before the turn of the century. Here are the boats, now moldering in the damp fall grass, that carried loved ones safely on the big lake.

The blackened chimney, all that remains of the "South Cottage" after a government crew thoughtlessly let a fireplace fire get away from them, evokes bittersweet memories of other days. It stands brooding guard over the vanishing trail to the south side of the island, where bits of copper could be extracted, with great effort, from the native rock.

There is the fish house, filled with long unused nets, floats and anchors, still pungent with the odors denoting its purpose. The insistent cries of the sea gulls fill the air. Perched expectantly on the ridge of the roof, they await food that does not come, since commercial fishing is no longer allowed at Isle Royale.

We at *Lake Superior Magazine* were privileged to receive copies of Betty's letters to her family. Nearly book length, they are a tender and very revealing look at our America of the 1930s and the 1940s, when wealth might be a new flour sack curtain over the dish cupboard.

The stories range from the terror of a Lake Superior storm, as seen from a small boat through the eyes of a little girl, to the hauntingly expressive description of nightfall on Isle Royale. From planked fish picnics on the Fourth of July to the tearful farewell of returning to school in the fall. In a word, the story is beautiful.

Originally appeared in Lake Superior Magazine, *November/December 1987*

Good Night, *Skipper Sam II*

Whether you are buttoning up the lake cabin or draining and winterizing your recreational vehicle, we know winter is not far away. The mind fills with varied thoughts associated with such a task, but pleasant memories try to offset the sheer hard work involved.

Skipper Sam II, our nautical magic carpet, is almost 30 years old this fall. Each year as I move the boat toward the lift-out well, memories flood my mind, rushing by as *Skipper Sam* resigns herself to another winter in the cradle. *Sam* has long known that winters trigger careful reading of boating magazines and studied analysis of yacht broker offerings. To make sure I don't forget her, she responds as well as a trained cat as we maneuver into the lift-out dock.

Joel Johnson, owner of Lakehead Boat Basin, is waiting. His Travel Lift is ready, and soon *Skipper Sam II* is nestled in her cradle for the season. Just one boat of a long parade that Joel cares for each fall and spring. His services are a vital link in our chosen avenue of relaxation.

Climbing the tall ladder to get aboard her gives me a strange feeling. Almost the first item I notice to put away is the American flag we fly from the stern. We fly the real flag, with 50 stars, not the U.S. Yacht Ensign, which has a blue field with a circle of stars and a fouled anchor. We have also elected to show our United States Power Squadron membership by flying the Duluth Squadron pennant, rather than the U.S. Power Squadron flag.

Much of our summer cruising is done on Canadian waters, where the only flag legally displayed on an American craft should be the U.S. flag. Carefully folded, the flag joins quite a library in our flag drawer, lying next to the smaller bright red-and-white Canadian flag we proudly display on our starboard (right) antenna when in Canadian waters. Almost, but not quite obscured under all of these flags is a small square yellow flag. Just to notice it brings a grin and finally a big chuckle!

Bob Lang, although no longer with us, is also chuckling, I think, and he doesn't even know why.

Our visits to Canada have spanned almost 30 years. We always make sure our Canadian flag is displayed with the point of the

The end of another wonderful season of boating finds the Skipper Sam II being hauled out for the winter at Lakehead Boat Basin in Duluth, Minnesota. Jan Biga photo.

maple leaf UP, and have always carried a yellow, or quarantine flag, which we display below the Canadian flag until cleared into Canada by customs.

True maritime custom and regulation dictates that a visitor fly a yellow rectangular flag under the visiting nation flag – a flag of pratique. It means we recognize that we are in another country, but have not cleared Customs and Immigration.

For years, our yellow flag was just a crudely trimmed patch of yellow fabric, laced in place temporarily, just to show we knew the custom. Longtime crew member Bob Lang, well known to our Canadian friends as the source of fabulous spaghetti sauce, went through a ritual of wincing almost to the point of oozing blood each time the tattered banner was displayed.

Coming to Lake Superior from the wilds of the Fox River and Kaukauna, Wisconsin, he knew proper boating etiquette. The challenge of educating us misfits must have seemed almost an even trade for another boat ride.

Came the inevitable bulky Christmas present from Kaukauna, obviously wrapped by Bob's lovely wife, Cosette, long skilled at covering Bob's tracks. After much unwrapping, a smart and fully tailored "Quarantine" flag appeared, regaling a degree of splendor not often noted in the upper reaches of Lake Superior.

A moment of silence fell upon us. This new flag instantly converted the rest of our flag collection into oddly colored rags. Smuggling it aboard so the other flags wouldn't notice was indeed a challenge, but the dark of night conspired with fog to aid us in the task. We considered just dropping it into the bay, but after recalling Bob's advanced age and infirm condition, the new flag came aboard. Bob would have noted its absence, and an unhappy Bob was a German unchained!

In that quiet boat, on this haul-out day, memories flooded my mind. With a smile, I felt Bob Lang around me, as were Stan Salmi and so many others who just enjoyed being a part of *Skipper Sam II*.

Suddenly we were crossing from the upper Canadian islands of Lake Superior toward Isle Royale, I think the year was 1986. Every weather report confirmed good sea conditions, so we discussed just "where in the Hell" these five-foot waves were coming from, and just what had happened to the visibility, which now seemed less than a half mile.

Approaching the northeast corner of Isle Royale in tough sea conditions is somewhat of a "chancy" adventure. Far offshore reefs blend with the sometimes visible Canoe Rocks that claimed both the *Congdon* and the *Emperor*.

Bob Lang used radar to gain bearings to land masses such as Blake Point on the northeastern end of Isle Royale, while I steered the boat. Carefully and quietly he laid out the bearings on our chart, confirming the indicated degrees with another look at the radar. Adjusting courses to his calculations, we finally gained the safety and relatively calm water of Amygdaloid Channel, which led us to the safety of McCargoe Cove.

We've discussed Bob Lang in the past. Readers might wonder how such a tidy and carefully maintained vessel as *Skipper Sam II* would let some unwashed soul from central Wisconsin aboard, much less as crew. Alas, 1977 was a tough year. Offers of a warm bunk and good food were for naught. Daughter Cindy finally sent a scrawled resume from Wisconsin, noting, "He says he has some boating experience."

"Despite that," she pointed out, "he has a wonderful wife."

Well, wouldn't you know. Bob and Cose showed up! Soon the boat's windows were washed to the point you could not tell they contained glass, dishes were clean and neatly stacked, coffee cups bleached of all coffee stains. We were surprised that we found both of them to be comfortable company. To their surprise (according to Cosette) they found they could even stand US!

Over the years, Cose, as we call Cosette, and Bob became first crew on our summertime adventures.

Bob and Cosette Lang were two of the sparkling diamonds on the necklace that is boating. Bob quietly added to my boating knowledge as we shared trips on our boat and theirs. Anticipating retirement, Bob bought a 45-foot live-aboard cruiser in Wisconsin, which they named the *Cosette L.*, taking it in stages to North Fort Myers, Florida.

As spring approached, they cruised the Intercoastal Waterway of the East Coast, winding up one year in Chesapeake Bay, where the boat was stored for the summer. I had the fun of joining them for a portion of that particular cruise and will never forget meeting head-on with a nuclear submarine just north of Florida.

Bob and Cose made the boat their winter home for three years, when finally Cosette announced that it was time for "more room, more room and more room." Bob often was accused of hearing only what he wanted to, but he got that message in record time. Soon they were relaxing in a new condominium.

I find myself envious of the wintering lifestyle they had in Punta Gorda, Florida. While I drain engine coolants and winterize our water system with "drinkable anti-freeze," Bob was faced with pulling his boat and cleaning off all the barnacles. I stow all the fenders, lines and cover the upper bridge, reflecting on his attention to the "Hurricane Watch," just a part of wintering in Florida.

With a pat of appreciation, *Skipper Sam II* nestles in for a winter's nap. Within her are the U.S. and Canadian flags – and also one brightly colored quarantine flag.

All will be there in the spring.

Originally appeared in Lake Superior Magazine, *October/November 1995*

INDEX

179

181

Books

Emanations of Silver Islet and *Further Emanations of Silver Islet.* Bill MacDonald, 1995, Porphry Press, Thunder Bay, Ontario, Canada

Ingeborg's Isle Royale. Ingeborg Holte, 1984, Women's Times Publishing, Grand Marais, Minnesota

Isle Royale National Park. Jim DuFresne, 1991, The Mountaineers, Seattle, Washington

Once Upon an Isle. Howard Sivertson, 1992, Wisconsin Folk Museum, Mount Horeb, Wisconsin

Prehistoric Copper Mining in the Lake Superior Region. Roy W. Drier and Octave J. Du Temple, 1961, Calumet, Michigan

Seven Iron Men. Paul deKruif, 1929, Harcourt Brace and Co., New York, New York

Shipwrecks of Isle Royale National Park. Daniel Lenihan et al, 1994, Lake Superior Port Cities Inc., Duluth, Minnesota

Shipwreck of the Mesquite. Frederick Stonehouse, 1991, Lake Superior Port Cities Inc., Duluth, Minnesota

Silver Islet: Striking it Rich in Lake Superior. Elinor Barr, 1988, Natural Heritage/Natural History Inc., Toronto, Ontario, Canada

Tales of the Old North Shore. Howard Sivertson, 1996, Lake Superior Port Cities Inc., Duluth, Minnesota

Wonderful Power: Ancient Copper Working in the Lake Superior Basin. 1999, Susan R. Martin, Wayne University Press, Detroit, Michigan

Magazine

"Burning Desire: Search for Early U.P. Man," James Paquette, Dec./Jan. 1996, Volume 17 Issue 6, *Lake Superior Magazine* p.22

Film

"Drowning in Dreams," documentary film on the yacht *Gunilda*, Canadian Film Board, Toronto, Canada

James R. Marshall comes to the publishing world in rather a round-about fashion. Being a natural storyteller, a scuba diver, a history buff, a diehard entrepreneur, the last owner of salvage rights to the sunken steamer *America* on Isle Royale and an avid boater, he got interested in the start-up of a regional magazine called *Lake Superior Port Cities* in an office adjacent to his own in his hometown of Duluth, Minnesota.

Twenty years later, as co-owner, he remains vitally interested and involved in that enterprise, which evolved into *Lake Superior Magazine*. His "Lake Superior Journal" appears in each issue and consistently ranks as a favorite with readers. It is often the first place where issues are raised relating to the welfare of Lake Superior, its people and the wide range of enterprise associated with the big lake.

This book is a compilation of the early columns from the "Lake Superior Journal." But readers will not get far into the book before they encounter other important personas that are regular players in Jim's tales – his wife, Jan Biga, the people who accompany as boat crews on his adventures and, quite prominently, both the original *Skipper Sam* and the *Skipper Sam II*, the latter a comfortable boat that has served since 1976 as a trusty magic carpet to many of these adventures.

And "adventure" is really the correct definition for these tales, for even the warm memories of departed friends contain elements that add excitement to the stories.

When he isn't out meeting Lake Superior's people or chasing information of interest to him, Jim serves as District Sales Manager for Columbia Steel Castings Co., a manufacturer supplying specialty manganese steel and iron wear parts to mines, power plants, scrap metal processors and other businesses. He and wife, Jan, make their home in Duluth.